Sophie du Pont

A Young Lady in America

An early watercolor (before 1827) by Sophie du Pont.

Sophie du Pont

A Young Lady in America

Sketches, Diaries, & Letters
1823–1833

by Betty-Bright Low and Jacqueline Hinsley

Harry N. Abrams, Inc., Publishers, New York

For David and Curt

Editor: Ruth Eisenstein

Designer: Carol Ann Robson

Library of Congress Cataloging-in-Publication Data

du Pont, Sophie.
  Sophie du Pont, a young lady in America.

  1. Du Pont, Sophie—Diaries.   2. Du Pont, Sophie—
Correspondence.   3. Du Pont, Sophie—Notebooks, sketch-
books, etc.   4. Du Pont family.   5. Delaware—Biography.
I. Low, Betty-Bright P.   II. Hinsley, Jacqueline.
III. Title.
CT275.D88247A3   1987   929'.2'0973   87–1452
ISBN 0–8109–1136–1

Published in 1987 by Harry N. Abrams, Incorporated, New York

Times Mirror Books

Printed and bound in the United States of America

Text copyright ©1987 Betty-Bright Low and Jacqueline Hinsley
Illustrations copyright ©1987 Hagley Museum and Library and
©1987 The Nemours Foundation

All the photography for this book (the Rembrandt Peale portrait
of Sophie du Pont excepted) is the work of Philip Pocock, New York.

The hand-marbled jacket paper, copyright © Dancing Inks, Olympia,
Washington, was created by Eileen Canning.

On the title page:

Rembrandt Peale. *Sophie du Pont.* 1831.

Oil on canvas, 29 1/8 x 24 3/8".

Hagley Museum and Library, Wilmington (on loan).

Courtesy of Mr. and Mrs. Henry E.I. du Pont.

Table of Contents

One day on the Hancopanian

Being a series of dialogues from Real Life.

With Illustrations. — A.D. 1827

Dramatis Personæ.

Alfred   Mama
Euelopius   Victorine
Staucatius   Tat
Sprol   Soph
Alexis   Mela & Nice

       Dwarf

Dedicated.

To the most noble and charming Lady
Mary Augusta Nepomucina Lamont
By her devoted friend   The Author.

Scene 1st

Vic and Tat in bed — Enter Dwarf —
1st Dwarf. "Ladies, the breakfast is just coming up."
2nd Tat (jumping up) "Oh my! why didn't you tell us sooner"
3rd Vic (yawning) "Well. I suppose we'd best get up."

Scene 2nd. The dressing —

Soph's room. Soph by the fire. Mrs Waterman holding
her dress. In rush Vic and Tat — with their clothes —
1st Tat. "Oh dress me, Mrs Waterman dress me!"
2nd Vic.   (The breakfast bell rings without)
2nd Vic. "Ch! Ch! there the bell."
3rd Soph (in a despairing tone) "Now! there they are all!
and I won't be dressed to day!!!"

Scene 3d

The consequences of getting up late (i.e.)
a tête à tête with Staucatius
1st Staucatius 2nd Tat —
     (Both mute)

The pages of Sophie du Pont's booklet "One Day on the Tancopanican."
1827. Pencil and watercolor; each page c. 2 x 4".

AUTHORS' NOTES AND ACKNOWLEDGMENTS

Sophie's correspondence is voluminous; her closely written diaries and journals were a lifetime occupation. Our research was greatly facilitated by the discovery that Sophie's drawing was limited to a decade of her youth, 1823–1833. Since those years were also the decade of her brother Henry's education away from home, their correspondence has been a major source of documentation and is quoted more often than any other. Identification of the writer, recipient, and date of quoted letters is usually included in brackets following the quoted text, with first-name initial for Sophie and her immediate family (E for Eleuthera, Ev for Evelina).

The original orthography and punctuation have been retained in all quoted material, and translation has been kept to a minimum, since bilingualism is part of the charm of Sophie's idiom. Certain idiosyncracies characterize Sophie's epistles, for example her tendency to mark the end of a sentence with a dash, or not to mark it at all, and her consistent omission of one *l* from the word *squalling*. Otherwise, little consistency will be noted in her spelling, which reflects the less rigorous practice of the time.

The family name du Pont follows modern usage (du Pont for the family, Du Pont for the business). In the case of Samuel Francis Du Pont, United States Naval Registers have dictated the capitalization.

Sophie's comments and observations were not limited to her letters and other writings. They were inscribed also on the carics themselves, sometimes on the reverse side, and they appear here as the captions accompanying the illustrations; those written on the reverse side are indicated by [V°].

From more than 200 carics and drawings, 186 are reproduced in this volume. Originally we intended to publish only Sophie's caricatures, because they are so unlike the typical drawings of young ladies of her era. But to demonstrate the scope of her artistic interests, we have added a sampling of her natural history sketches and landscapes. Throughout, the dimensions of the drawings as reproduced vary slightly from the actual sizes of the originals, most of which measure about four by five inches.

This volume owes its existence to treasures in that wonderful archival category known as Miscellany. Almost half the sketches reproduced in the following pages were scattered through the papers of the daughters of Eleuthère Irénée du Pont in the du Pont family archives at the Hagley Museum and Library. Reunited with an equal number of drawings from another du Pont family repository, the Nemours Foundation, and documented by the contextual material from which they had been separated, they are presented here as a unit for the first time.

In a very real sense we are indebted to several generations of du Ponts with a strong commitment to the preservation of family papers and memorabilia. Many of the sketches and letters were found in the papers of Sophie and her sisters in the Henry Francis du Pont Collection of Winterthur Manuscripts, willed by Sophie herself to her brother Henry's son, Henry Algernon du Pont, whose consuming interest in family history prompted the bequest. Through him they went to his son Henry Francis, founder of the Henry Francis du Pont Winterthur Museum, and thence to Hagley. Other sketches were discovered in the manuscripts assembled at Longwood by Pierre S. du Pont, a grandson of Sophie's eldest brother, Alfred; Pierre's papers became the nucleus of Hagley's collections. One of the finest groups of caricatures, some two dozen drawings found in an ancient sewing table, was given to Hagley by Mrs. Jean Austin du Pont when we were well along in research for the book. They had been preserved through the family of William du Pont, Henry Algernon's younger brother. Two sizable groups of sketches were located in the collections at Nemours, home of the late Alfred Irénée du Pont, another grandson of Sophie's brother Alfred. Nearly sixty of them are mounted in an album on exhibit there. The discovery of the remaining forty or so sketches in an old safe at a late date caused great excitement and some dismay. Three dozen new caricatures to be documented and incorporated into the text!

Curator Ruth Linton not only made the sketches at Nemours available for study and photographing but took a personal interest in the project. Thomas S. Coldewey, Trustee of the Nemours Foundation, facilitated permission to publish from their collections. We are much indebted to them, and to the Foundation, for their generous cooperation.

Encouragement in the challenging process of matching letter and caricature came initially from Anthony F. C. Wallace, who had used Sophie's papers in the research for his *Rockdale*. Claudia Bushman, friend, author, and executive director of the Delaware Heritage Commission, took on the task of critiquing our first draft. Her perceptive comments pointed us early on in the direction the book eventually took.

We owe much to the vision of Walter J. Heacock and to his successor, Glenn Porter, director of the Hagley Museum and Library. And we could not have carried the book to completion without the steady support of a few colleagues, like Marjorie McNinch, whose familiarity with the manuscripts proved an invaluable asset. Through the expertise of photographer Charles Foote and the forbearance of colleagues Daniel T. Muir and Jon M. Williams, Sophie du Pont's sketches themselves "came to light," to use the language of that Old Gray Possum, Andrew Fountain. During the five years of research and writing, friends Mary Pitlick and Nancy Seaman loyally read and discussed various versions of Sophie's story. Vera Osborne, Ann McGurgan, Sarah Pierce, Margie O'Boyle, and Robin Bowers typed the manuscript.

Elisabeth Donaghy Garrett channeled the felicitous match of material and publisher. We are grateful, for she introduced us to Paul Gottlieb, a Francophile with a critical appreciation of the early American scene. We have been truly fortunate in his selection of editor Ruth Eisenstein and designer Carol Robson, who have shown remarkable sensitivity to the material while seeing Sophie's sketches, letters, and diaries through the press.

Wilmington, February 1987   *J.H. and B-B.L.*

DRAMATIS PERSONAE

❧ INHABS ❧

Vic, Sister
Victorine du Pont Bauduy, eldest daughter of Irénée and Sophie Dalmas du Pont, married Ferdinand Bauduy in 1813; widowed in 1814.

Lina
Evelina du Pont Bidermann, second du Pont daughter, married James Antoine Bidermann in 1816; first mistress of Winterthur.

Brother, Antoine
James Antoine Bidermann; managed the gunpowder manufactory after Irénée du Pont's death until Alfred du Pont became its head, in 1837.

Alf
Alfred Victor du Pont, eldest son of Irénée and Sophie Dalmas du Pont; head of the Du Pont Company 1837–1850.

Meta
Margaretta Lammot du Pont, Alfred's wife, and mistress of Nemours, their home after 1826.

Eleu, Tat, Tata
Eleuthera du Pont, third du Pont daughter, married Thomas Mackie Smith in 1834.

Soph, Sophia
Sophie Madeleine du Pont, youngest du Pont daughter, married her first cousin Samuel Francis Du Pont in 1833.

Harry, Hal, Corporal O'Possumtail, Marquis de Furioso
Henry du Pont, second du Pont son; graduated from West Point and served briefly in the United States Army before entering the powder business; headed the Du Pont Company 1850–1889.

Lily, Lil
Alexis Irénée du Pont, youngest du Pont son, married Joanna Maria Smith in 1836; killed in a powder explosion in 1857.

Sir Sprol, Uncle
Charles Dalmas, brother of Sophie Dalmas du Pont; foreman of the powder yard until injured in a powder explosion in 1818.

The Son & Heir
James Irénée Bidermann, only child of Evelina and Antoine, contemporary of Alexis.

The Youngies
Victorine, Emma Paulina, Irénée, Lammot (Alfred and Meta's children).

Lady Waters
Mrs. Waterman, seamstress.

Esculapius, Doctorus
Pierre Didier, physician who served by annual contract all the medical needs of the du Pont family and the powder mill workers and their families.

Starecatus
Jean Delages, Du Pont Company chemist, who lived in a garret room at Eleutherian Mills during his employment (1824–1830).

❧ OVERCREEKERS ❧

Charles
Charles Irénée du Pont, elder son of Victor and Josephine du Pont; became manager of the woolen mill at Louviers.

Frank
Samuel Francis Du Pont, second son of the Victor du Ponts; married Sophie du Pont in 1833; later an admiral in the United States Navy.

It is with great pleasure that I take up the pen to inform you of the birth of a little niece. She was born yesterday evening, and both Margaretta and her daughter are well. The baby is called Victorine she has dark eyes and hair and is very pretty—I cannot tell you how glad we all are but I expect you will be equally so. Little Victorine does nothing but sleep now, but I expect she will be much improved in September. Lilly is delighted, it is something so new to have a niece!!!!!!!! [S to H, 14 August 1825]

Julia
Julia du Pont, second daughter of the Victor du Ponts; married Irvine Shubrick, officer in the United States Navy, in 1824.

Ella, Lady Bristlebrow, Lieutenant Skearquick
Gabrielle Josephine du Pont, granddaughter of the Victor du Ponts; married William Breck in 1836.

The Youngies
Thomas and Frank Shubrick, Julia and Irvine's sons.

Tinshanks
Gaspard Tranchant, native of France, proprietor of a Brandywine cotton mill.

Great Gibbon
Joshua Gibbon, teacher in both night school and Brandywine Manufacturers' Sunday School.

❧ FRIENDS AND NEIGHBORS ❧

The Gray Possum
Andrew Fountain, kept a general store by the Brandywine ferry.

Knight of Rockdale, Val de Peñas
John Smith Phillips, a founding member of the Franklin Institute of Philadelphia; an unsuccessful suitor of Sophie du Pont, he never married.

Pruderino, Prudencio
Prudencio Santander, classmate of Alexis du Pont at Mr. Bullock's school in Wilmington; frequent visitor at Eleutherian Mills before returning to his native Chile.

Lotta
Charlotte Busti Cazenove of Alexandria, closest friend of Sophie du Pont; attended Mme. Grelaud's school in Philadelphia.

Sir Cicero Crumb of Crumb Hall
Alexander Stuart Read, West Point graduate and Wilmington lawyer; lived in a house called Tusculum.

Tom, Lord George Fitzallan
Thomas Mackie Smith, son of Francis Gurney Smith and his wife, Elizabeth; studied medicine at the University of Pennsylvania and was resident physician at the Philadelphia Hospital; married Eleuthera du Pont in 1834.

Joan, Lady Joan
Joanna Maria Smith, sister of Thomas Mackie Smith, married Alexis du Pont in 1836.

Dick
Richard Smith, son of Francis Gurney and Elizabeth Smith, and classmate of Henry du Pont at West Point.

A Family Party

We cut a ridiculous figure enough. Imagine Lina on Annette with Paulina on her lap & Victorine à califourchon behind holding the back of the saddle with both her little hands. Her coat floating over Annette's back so that the animal's tail descended from its folds! . . . Then Sister, myself, Sophie, Meta, Mrs Taylor, & Th^os as a rear guard, a little en arriere, while between the beast & us Brother walked waving the enormous wand of power with which he manages her donkeyship—

[E to H, 16 January 1830]

Clem
Clementina Smith, daughter of Richard Somers Smith of Philadelphia, later of Lenni.

Nora
Elenora Adelaide Lammot, daughter of Daniel Lammot and his first wife; frequently visited her elder sister Margaretta on the Brandywine.

Mary
Mary Augusta Lammot, sister of Meta and Nora, also a frequent visitor to the Brandywine; married Thomas Hounsfield in 1832.

Polly, Pol
Mary Edith Simmons, daughter of a neighboring Brandywine farmer; ward of James Antoine Bidermann after her father's death.

Eliza, Elisa
Eliza J. Schlatter, daughter of William and Catherine Schlatter; married Theophilus Parsons Chandler.

Lady Barcatus
Mary Alletta Hedrick Belin, wife of Augustus Belin, Du Pont Company accountant.

The Architect
William Boyd, carpenter for Irénée du Pont.

Ursa Major and Ursa Minor
Brothers William and Evans Young of Rockland.

❧ PETS ❧

Dogs
Bevis, Flora, Miss, Major, Cupid, Juba, Caesar, Pallas

Lallah

Cats
Lallah, Pluto, Proserpine, Rousseau, Lady Lex, Cloe, Lady Erminia, Abra, Griffon, Catalina, Nox, Tigrane

Deer
Azore, Zelia, Evora, Hector, Zamor, Fanny

Donkey
Annette

Birds
Pol, Count, Tom, Zize Pampan

Horses
Sidney, Ferris, and Mr. Phillips's steeds Mazeppa and Wildfire

Note
Research has not yet revealed any names assigned to White Rat, flying squirrels, pigs, or fowl; nor were hummingbirds named despite their regular visits in through the parlor window.

INTRODUCTION

*A*dramatic chronicle of youth and family in the Early Republic is provided by the letters, diaries, and sketches of Sophie Madeleine du Pont (1810–1888). During her teen years Sophie found a vivid means of self-expression—caricature. Her "carics," as Sophie called them, were intended for a knowing audience—her brothers, sisters, and close friends. More than a century and a half later, they present an intimate glimpse of a young woman growing up in a rural manufacturing environment. When Sophie drew her carics, the du Pont name, so well known in the annals of American business, was new in this country.

Sophie's father, Eleuthère Irénée du Pont (1771–1834), had entered the United States on January 3, 1800, after a harrowing voyage across the Atlantic from France with his wife, their children Victorine, Evelina, and Alfred, and other family members. Following a brief sojourn in New Jersey and a return trip to France to gain expertise and obtain equipment for a projected venture in the manufacture of gunpowder, in 1802 he brought his family to Delaware. There, four miles north of Wilmington, he settled on the banks of the Brandywine Creek. The number of his progeny grew to seven with the births of Eleuthera, Sophie, Henry, and Alexis, and his gunpowder enterprise—the ancestor of the industrial giant E. I. du Pont de Nemours & Co.—flourished.

It was the Brandywine, roaring powerfully through a rock-strewn valley toward the Delaware River, that had attracted Irénée du Pont to the site. Along its banks, as along other streams and rivers, a new layer of society was emerging, a manufacturing class intent on building an industrial America. Irénée was well suited to join this group, for he shared the belief that manufacturing was essential to the future of the nation, and he had the requisite stamina and perseverance. His gunpowder establishment, which he named Eleutherian Mills, ranged along sixty-five acres of the riverbank. To keep vigil over his manufacturing operation, Irénée situated his house on a bluff overlooking the mills and kept a speaking trumpet handy to call down instructions to his workmen, most of whom spoke only English, a language Irénée could hardly understand. His office was just inside, on the first floor, so that the house was the very pulse of the growing industrial establishment as well as the family seat.

Despite the steady growth of his business, Irénée du Pont was never out of debt and always short of capital. He spent much of his time journeying from banks in Philadelphia to banks in Baltimore seeking the renewal of notes. His struggle to become established in his new country was compounded by a bitter dispute with his original partner and by the financial demands of his European stockholders. His children, then, saw their father constantly fatigued, and they were keenly aware of the sacrifices he made for their well-being. They knew that to gain support for his business Papa forced himself to meet people and take a public role though social gatherings were uncongenial to his nature. Somewhat moody and reticent, even shy, partly because of sensitivity about a birthmark on his left cheek, he favored simplicity in his home, and the warmth of a close family circle.

Irénée's preference for simple country living was shared by his wife, Sophie Dalmas du Pont (1775–1828). Like her husband, she was of a retiring disposition. Only sixteen years old when she fell in love with Irénée du Pont and married him, she had proved to be an excellent manager of the family farm in France. She did as well on the Brandywine; following Irénée's instructions, she managed the powder yards in his absence besides supervising her growing family and boarding the bachelor work force. But she never fully mastered the language of her adopted country.

Their fourth and youngest daughter, the second child born in America, inherited her parents' shyness. She was named for her mother, whom she resembled.

> *This new Sister of ours came into the world day before yesterday at 8 o'clock in the Evening–This little girl is so very little that I cant tell you anything else about her–people say she is very handsome–a thing however which has been averred and regretted is that she is the only one in the family who has not a dimpled Chin–I know you will be sorry of this and so is mama.*
>
> [V to Ev, 20 September 1810]

Later Sophie did develop the du Pont trait, and by the time she was drawing her carics she was five feet two inches tall and weighed 105 pounds, according to the scales in the powder yards.

Sophie and her siblings all learned English, but French was the language of the du Pont home. Holidays were celebrated in the French manner; French frugality dictated the season for fires in the grates and the meticulous entries in the household record books; French garden style was reflected in the parterres between the house and the orchard; French mourning customs prevailed whenever there was a death at Eleutherian Mills. In evidence too were the close ties to the French Enlightenment of the family patriarch, Pierre Samuel du Pont de Nemours (1739–1817). "Bon Papa," as little Sophie called him, bequeathed to his younger son, Irénée, his deist convictions, his intellectual curiosity, and his reverence for the land. Neither Irénée nor Sophie sought to impose these values on their children, but young Sophie, her brothers, and her sisters were all encouraged to appreciate the world of nature around them and to seize every opportunity to increase their knowledge of it.

The cosmopolitan ambience of Eleutherian Mills offered another kind of learning experience. From the time of his arrival in the United States, Papa had had influential friends, through Bon Papa and through his brother Victor. Du Pont de Nemours had supported the American cause even before the War of Independence, since he knew first Franklin and later Jefferson in Paris. Uncle Victor had served as French consul in Charleston and had worked tirelessly to secure the release of American ships seized by the French during the Quasi-War. Both men had given invaluable support to the American government during delicate stages of the Louisiana Purchase negotiations. Then, as Papa's business expanded and he gained a reputation as a promoter of manufactures, a steady stream of nationally known personages sought him out. While Sophie was growing up, there were visits from diplomat James Bayard, journalist Hezekiah Niles, and Whig leader Henry Clay, in addition to numerous local politicians. She recalled her father's writing home, "Get your bonnets washed . . . !" to announce that President James Monroe would come and tour the mills in 1817.

Sophie also remembered vividly the visit of General Lafayette in the summer of 1825. He was one of the many visitors from France who made their way to Eleutherian Mills. The Gallic hospitality they encountered delighted them, for Papa always took time to receive his countrymen and to help those who called upon him for aid. He introduced one such guest, Guillaume Tell Poussin, to Benjamin Latrobe, who was looking for an assistant in carrying out L'Enfant's design for Washington, D.C.

Originally the lively French community in nearby Wilmington had been a consideration in Irénée du Pont's settling on the Brandywine. In the 1820s, when Sophie began drawing her carics, many of those early French families had left the area, but by then the du Ponts were accepted in their neighborhood. In the years in between, there had been times when suspicion was directed at them, as foreigners and as producers of gunpowder. During the War of 1812 the feeling was intense, especially among their Quaker neighbors, when the Brandywine was declared a primary British target. In response, the du Ponts and their workmen helped organize the Brandywine Rangers to keep watch in the valley. The women and children watched the Rangers drill daily, and among Sophie's earliest recollections was the echo of their trumpets calling from both sides of the creek, up and down the valley. Uncle Charles Dalmas, Mama's brother, who lived at Eleutherian Mills, painted the Rangers' flag, a beehive on white silk with the motto "Bees in Peace, Hornets in War."

Sophie had a special reason to recall that many military men came to the house during this time. One, a Lieutenant Prevost, presented her with a handsome red travel case lined in delicately stenciled pink silk with a full complement of sewing equipment. Years later Sophie set this note inside it:

This nécessaire was given to me when I was three years old, by Lt. A. Prevost— He was an officer at Camp Du Pont, during the war with England in 1813–14—And was very much in love with sister Evelina—which he received too little encouragement to avow openly, but tried to pay her attentions thro' me—He professed therefore to be my devoted sweetheart, allowed me to play with his epaulets. . . . I have but a faint recollection of him—blended with gold tinsel—his epaulets having made a deeper impression on me than himself—nevertheless I always kept & valued this present of his—It made me feel myself of much consequence to own something so splendid & valuable. . . .

During that era of unabashed patriotism, Papa expanded his gunpowder mills, cotton and woolen mills started production, and what had been an isolated wilderness along the Brandywine grew into an industrial community. In December 1815 Sophie's cousin Samuel Francis Du Pont received his appointment as a midshipman in the United States Navy. Cousin Frank's family—his mother and father, Josephine and Victor du Pont, his elder brother, Charles, his sisters, Amelia and Julia, and their families—were overcreekers, that is, they lived across the Brandywine, at Louviers. The entire du Pont family was elated at Frank's joining the Navy, the most glamorous arm of the military after the war, and Sophie shared the general delight. More than a decade later, when her own closest friend and playmate, her brother Henry, received his appointment to the United States Military Academy at West Point, her joy was unbounded. In play and in daydream she was fascinated by the military—a predilection evident in the language of her carics. Her preoccupation proved contagious, for her closest friends easily fell under the sway of military terminology and marched to Sophie's tune.

Sophie's circle of friends was drawn in part from the manufacturing and farming families of the neighborhood, like the Gilpins, with their paper mill at Kentmere, and the Simmonses, who farmed the property later known as Winterthur. Most prominent in her carics, though, are the sons and daughters of Papa's business acquaintances—Lammots, Smiths, and Cazenoves. Both the Smiths and the Cazenoves were devout Episcopalians, extremely active in the Sunday School movement that was blossoming throughout the country. Introspective as she was, Sophie was strongly influenced by them in matters of religion and fully embraced the current evangelistic fervor. Yet, faithful to her Huguenot ancestry, she abhorred ostentation in church:

I like simplicity in a place of worship–In the house where we should go to worship and not to gaze. [S to H, 30 April 1833]

Theological works were a cornerstone of her reading. However, her literary taste was wide-ranging, and though she had only four months of formal schooling she was amazingly informed on many subjects—entomology, ornithology, horticulture, botany, Greek and Roman classics, English history and literature, French history and literature, Spanish literature, politics, and current events. She traveled the world in books. Her unremitting search for learning was very natural in view of Papa's consistent encouragement of intellectual curiosity in his children, daughters included. Sophie's natural timidity and her modest demeanor kept the full extent of her attainments hidden from casual acquaintants.

Unfortunately, Sophie found some of her special interests thwarted by social realities. Women had no vote, and too impassioned a conversation on politics was considered unseemly in a lady. Only in her diaries and her letters to her brother could she fully vent her feelings on national issues, and even to Henry she felt obliged to excuse herself for expressing strong opinions concerning the national election:

> *I expect you will be thunderstruck at the idea of my meddling in politics, and still more at my being on the Adams side–But it is because he protects manufactures, in which we have the best possible right to feel interested as it is from them we derive our subsistence.* [S to H, 1828]

An inveterate reader of the magazines, newspapers, and pamphlets that filled the closets at Eleutherian Mills, she also listened intently to the spirited political talk of the du Pont men on such subjects as protectionism, abolition, temperance, and the Indians. Sophie felt free to question the wisdom of an expedition against the Indians in the guise of reporting local concerns to an absent member of the family:

> *I should be extremely pained if ordered to fight an enemy whose cause I would feel to be just, & whose situation so every way entitled to excite sympathy & interest–Oppressed, tormented in every way, treated with injustice beyond endurance, these poor remnants of a once powerful & glorious nation yet remember that they are men & take up arms in self defence–They are weak & few compared to our armies, & unskilled in war, unprovided with our resources–These are the people, these the foe that the flower of our land would think it glorious & heroick to butcher. . . . I must say, I cant understand this–* [S to H, 26 July 1832]

Sophie was no revolutionary. Far from it, she took great pains to keep her actions and her manner always "proper." Nonetheless she felt a certain ambivalence concerning the role of women in the society of her day. Her French heritage was at odds with the realities of her American existence. Prefiguring what Alexis de Tocqueville would write two decades later, her Aunt Josephine, Sophie's future mother-in-law, viewed the issue in terms of the marked differences between the English and French cultures. The English granted freedom to their young women, she observed, and then restricted the matron to a throne of domesticity. The French reversed the sequence by sheltering the youth, then freeing the matron to shine in society and to act in partnership with her husband. Sophie's parents adhered to this French tradition, but their daughters sought to be Americanized, and thus to follow the prevalent British pattern. Victorine, Evelina, and Eleuthera, their outlook shaped by their peers and teachers at school, were satisfied to cultivate perfection in the domestic arts at the expense of their intellectual inclinations.

Sophie, although she emulated her sisters, was less willing to pay such a price, and she was reluctant to relinquish the freedom of choice that her youth afforded her. She sought to delay as long as she could the assumption of the mature role that confronted her. When she and Henry parted in 1828 at the start of his last year at Mt. Airy Military Lyceum in Germantown, she had a clear insight into her brother's future and her own. She saw him becoming a "busy, active man," while she was "growing up to 'mournful woman.' " Content with her country surroundings, she did not anticipate a socially active role in later life, yet her quick mind and French background kept her from easily accepting the standard American female role of provisioning, housekeeping, and childbearing.

Whereas Papa and her brothers encouraged Sophie's intellectual growth, her sisters impressed upon her the obligations of domesticity. Victorine and Eleu together criticized their little sister's expression of her opinions whenever they deviated from accepted social patterns of the day. Sophie felt their disapproval profoundly. Outnumbered by her older sisters, she cloaked herself in humility and took the path of least resistance, but the conflict was not absent from her private thoughts:

> *Particularly do I feel impressed with sadness when looking on a little girl, I remember the lot of woman which is to be her destiny! . . . To be gifted with quick & sensitive feelings, with warm & passionate affections, with genius, with rare talents perchance—& all this to be crushed & wasted, & borne back upon the heart, till the bitter medecine works at length the healing of the soul.—And is not this blessed healing, this withdrawal of the affections from earth & fixing of them on eternal happiness, worth all that must be borne for it?—Doubtless far more—and yet I am sometimes tempted to think with the Indian woman who said "Let not my child be a girl, for very sad is the lot of woman!"* [DIARY, February 1838]

Sophie fully appreciated the highly developed intellect and literary skills of Hannah More, Felicia Hemans, and Maria Edgeworth. She helped sister Tat collect the autographs of distinguished women of the century, like Harriet Beecher Stowe, Florence Nightingale, and Fanny Kemble. When she encountered Dorothea Dix, famous activist for improved mental health facilities, at the Smiths' in Philadelphia, Sophie was moved to admiration:

> *Miss Dix is a plain, mild, unassuming lady, with a most sweet winning voice; gentle & unobtrusive & quiet, you would think her some meek spinster that never scarcely stirred from her threshold. But listen to her converse & you are conscious of being in the presence of a very superior person.* [DIARY, 9 May 1853]

Sophie could accept the fact that among her own close friends were rebels like Mary Gilpin, who defied convention by insisting on intellectual freedom. But for herself, she had no wish to forgo the acceptance and approbation of her family and the society in which she was comfortable.

Ultimately she chose to accept the conventional role of the American woman. As she grew older, she conformed faithfully to the prescribed duties. With Mama's patient prodding, reinforced by Victorine's demands for excellence, she had become competent in the domestic arts. Her true interests she pursued through her religious activities—reading, teaching, and contributing to missionary efforts—and through her letter writing. At her death it was noted: "An invalid, confined to the house, and often to her room, her ministering hands were never idle, and she carried on as wide a correspondence as a Secretary of State. Through her fine literary gifts, her love of nature, above all, through her quick sympathy, she touched life at many points, and the circle of her influence was always widening; there will be weeping for her in far off continents and in islands of the sea."

The years of Sophie's carics were her years of decision as well as the years of her maturing. Through her sketches she captured the exuberance and the reality of her family circle. In caricature she found the freedom to express herself. And by doing so she has given us an unforgettable verbal and visual image of everyday life in a manufacturing family in Jacksonian America, during the early years of our nation.

Charles Dalmas (attrib.). Irénée du Pont encounters a group of his workmen passing a jug among them. c. 1812. Ink and wash, 9³/₄ x 16¹/₂″.

Baroness Hyde de Neuville. Eleutherian Mills (house and refinery). c. 1817. Brown wash drawing, 7x9″.

SOPHIE'S CARICS

*T*here was a strong tradition of artistic expression on the banks of the Brandywine to encourage Sophie to draw. Her father's partner, Peter Bauduy, had set up his easel to paint the famous family merino ram, Don Pedro, when he designed the elaborate cherub-laden label for Uncle Victor's woolen mill. Before she was ten years old, Sophie had watched as the Baroness Hyde de Neuville, wife of the French ambassador to the United States, sketched Eleutherian Mills and a number of other finely detailed scenes of the Brandywine environs. She was just eleven when, in the summer of 1821, two French artist/naturalists—Auguste Plée and Charles Alexandre Lesueur—were guests at Eleutherian Mills and went sketching in the course of their visits. The following autumn, sister Tat began to take drawing lessons with Lesueur in Philadelphia, and Sophie eagerly followed suit some three years later. In the meantime, Lesueur came to stay with the du Ponts each summer, and Sophie traipsed along on many a sketching expedition before she began her formal studies in drawing, essential to the education of young ladies in the Early Republic.

Label by Peter Bauduy for woolen goods produced by Du Pont, Bauduy & Company. c. 1812.

Sophie du Pont. *The Kings of the Frogs and Mice.* 1823. Pencil, 6¹/₈ x 7⁵/₈″.

LA PREMIERE LEÇON DE MA JEUNESSE.

TO MISS ELEUTHERA DU PONT. this DRAWING is AFFECTIONATELY INSCRIBED

BY her FRIEND the DELINEATOR

In caricature, however, her mentor was undoubtedly her uncle Charles Dalmas, self-taught cartoonist of Brandywine personalities. With her sketches Sophie preserved an ink-wash drawing of merino sheep executed about 1823 under the tutelage of Uncle Charles and presented as a gift to Eleuthera. But the strongest single clue to his influence is his rendition of Irénée du Pont discovering an illicit work break among his powdermen. The framing of a specific amusing moment, the matching dialogue, the meager facial detail, the postures of the workmen, and the use of watercolor—all are echoed in Sophie's carics. The encouragement of her uncle provided a steady stimulus to the budding caricaturist.

Exactly when Sophie began producing her carics is uncertain. Her correspondence suggests that she was in her thirteenth year when, as a present for her friend and neighbor Polly Simmons, she drew "a picture of the kings of the frogs and mice" inspired by an English translation of Homer's *Batrachomyomachia (The Battle of the Frogs and Mice)*. Victorine insisted that Sophie refrain from drawing animals until Eleuthera came home from school "to give her regular lessons, deeming it useless to let her bétasser without knowing what she is about."

That same year Sophie produced for her brother Henry a tiny book of illustrated verse. The small size was characteristic of many of her early drawings, perhaps an indication of the nearsightedness that troubled her. After Vic gave her a pair of spectacles on New Year's Day in 1831, Sophie proclaimed that they seemed "to remove a veil from before my sight." Some months before, she had been upset at not getting a clear view of Benjamin West's celebrated painting *Christ Rejected* when it was displayed in Philadelphia.

> *What was my disappointment to find I could not distinguish a single feature, being so short sighted! . . . The painting I could not properly judge of, even if I had been competent to do so, which I am not—on account of my short-sightedness—It is very large indeed, and well worth seeing—* [S to H, 13 May 1830]

In 1823, when Vic and Tat began editing a family newspaper, "The Tancopanican Chronicle" (Tancopanican being the Indian name for the Brandywine), Sophie was not part of the editorial effort. Her response to her sisters' partnership was to produce her own Tancopanican drawings. Entitled "Scenes on the Tancopanican," they were numbered and stitched together; two booklets of the scenes, both in color, are extant. These early sketches, readily differentiated from her more sophisticated later ones, are flat, faltering in execution, and poorly painted. Her first drawings of male figures lacked perspective. However, by 1830, when suitor John Phillips came calling, Sophie had learned to proportion all her figures to appear more active and lifelike.

When the idea of a caricature presented itself, Sophie made either a rough sketch or a quick jotting, with stick figures, to be developed later. From references to her well-documented sketch of a Quaker judge inveighing against General Jackson, it is certain that Sophie outlined this particular caric en route to school in 1825 and sent it home to be tinted by Tat. How many other drawings were completed, then later watercolored, is a matter for speculation. In 1827, Sophie's booklet "One Day on the Tancopanican" was executed both in pencil and in watercolor. In it she roughed out the entire series before polishing her drawings.

From the very first years of her sketching, Sophie seems to have grouped her carics much in the manner of the comic strips that were to appear a half century later. And the number of surviving single scenes suggests that additional series once existed or were planned.

By her own account, Sophie amused herself at Mrs. Grimshaw's school in the spring of 1825 by drawing "a series illustrating the manners and customs at Mrs. Grims," which apparently has been lost. She may also have completed a book of carics alluded to by Victorine in 1825 while attending a court session in New Castle, Delaware, with Polly Simmons, who wrote to Sophie on April 24:

I amused myself by looking at the lawyers who were by the by the most tremendous ugly set of men I ever saw particularly one who had on a dark green coat with a light green colour to it he sat with his arms hanging over one of the benches your sister whispered to me "I wish Sophie was here she would find so many excellent caricatures for her book."

Later Sophie contemplated a cartoon series based on her reading of the memoirs of the Duc de Sully.

I am greatly pleased with Sully's memoirs, they are so full of ludicrous anecdotes that I am constantly bursting out a laughing as I read. [s to h, 10 December 1830]

Victorine confirmed that

Sophie has met with several very amusing anecdotes in Sully's <u>Memoirs</u>, *she is going to draw a series of caricatures to illustrate them.* [v to e, 7 December 1830]

A pencil sketch of about the same date illustrating Sully's chilly accommodations at the Château of Anet in France is proof that she did indeed undertake to translate the Duc's written adventures into caricature, but no

"I was conducted into a vast chamber, all shining with marble, but so naked, and so cold, that I could neither get heat nor sleep in a bed where the short narrow silk curtains, a single slight coverlid, and damp sheets, were sufficient to benumb one, even in the midst of summer. Not able to continue in bed, I rose, and thought to secure myself against the inconveniences of my damp lodging, by making a fire; but I could find no other wood to burn than green walnut and juniper, which it was impossible to kindle."

other Sully caric has survived. Sophie continued to group her efforts when it was appropriate, but most of the carics stand as individual pieces, designed to convey the comedy of a particular incident.

Sophie's subjects are usually recognizable. The classic cartoon device of exaggerated likeness was well within the range of her talent. Figures most likely copied from contemporary cartoons in 1826 demonstrate her familiarity with the cartoonist's technique. But she preferred not to copy. As a result, without exception the most frequently represented and the most clearly identifiable characters in Sophie's drawings are people to whom she reacted with strong feelings. Physical anomaly she could readily dismiss with a single statement like "Phebus! What a nose!" But she was intolerant of those who "put on airs" or behaved in what she perceived to

be an affected manner. She unfailingly satirized those with inflated ideas of their own importance. So the superior stance of her suitor John Phillips earned his frequent portrayal in her carics as a man without a head, or a man towering so gigantically above others that he appears to have no head.

In contrast, the Company chemist Jean Delages, dubbed Starecatus, is always drawn with an oversized head on a shortened body. Sophie's resentment of his presence in the home accounts for her unflattering rendition and the humiliating situations in which she sketched him. With pear peelings falling on his head, held at bay by a motley pack of dogs, or defending himself from pet deer by means of a broom, Starecatus looks foolish indeed!

A more subtle treatment is reserved for sister Victorine, who is often depicted as unpleasant. She is also shown as out of control, when in fact she ruled the household. At the same time, Sophie's warm affection for her friend Lotta and brother-in-law Bidermann inspired consistently sympathetic portrayals in her sketches. Paradoxically, some of the individuals closest to Sophie appear rarely or not at all in her carics. Since Henry was away at school during the decade of her drawings and Cousin Frank was often at sea, their absence from most of the sketches is predictable. Papa does not appear in any of the collected carics, and Mama is drawn but once, in one of the earlier Tancopanican booklets, where she bears a striking resemblance to young Sophie in her self-portraits.

The caricaturist herself is prominent in the drawings, most frequently in the role of observer. Sophie, recognizable by her remarkably round cheeks and invariably bemused expression, is seldom the focal point of the action. She avoids center stage, even in *Preparations for a Wedding* (her own), where, by design, sister Eleuthera's adornment is the center of interest.

A study of the many scenes in which Sophie included herself leaves no doubt of her satisfaction with her world and her place in it. That world was a world without violence, a world of quiet humor, of daily chores, of rural pleasures. It was a world of family closeness and friendly laughter. It was essentially a world of youth, Sophie's youth, frozen in time and perfection through her sketches. Sophie idealizes it in a romantic style remi-

Conjugal Felicity

After you left us, Sophy, I & Alfred stationed ourselves in the parlour where we sat all morning but as Mama was with us constantly not out of the room five minutes, I found it impossible to work at my cap. Alexis said his lesson, read, & wrote very well, Sophy drew, & wrote & sewed as usual and as Alfred was with us almost-all day it passed very pleasantly though very quietly for Sophy & I are both mutes.

[Meta to V, December 1824]

niscent of her favorite novelist, Sir Walter Scott. The landscapes and inhabitants of the sketches are remapped, renamed. The Brandywine Creek is the Tancopanican; a hillside glade by the river is Veolan Bower. A Delaware farming and manufacturing establishment is peopled with knights and ladies from the Age of Chivalry. Uncle Charles magically becomes Sir Sprol. Lawyer Alexander Read of Tusculum attends a tea fight (contemporary slang for tea party) as Sir Cicero Crumb of Crumb Hall, and John Phillips arrives on his spirited mount Wildfire as the Knight of Rockdale. The caricaturist works in her attic hideaway room, Castle Blue.

An essential part of the caricature has traditionally been its language, either dialogue within the drawing or explanatory labeling without. By casting the more mundane happenings of daily life in the language of a bygone era and in another land, a fictional one at that, the imaginative young caricaturist heightens the incongruity and thereby the humor of her drawings. After Henry went to West Point, military jargon invaded the caric dialogue. Young ladies marched to the bathhouse as the Lavatory Company, Alfred's house was temporarily renamed Fortress Monroe, and the young ladies themselves assumed military rank.

Drawn for the entertainment of family and close friends, the carics reflect the bilingualism of Sophie's generation in the du Pont family. The joy of word games, puns, and double entendres in two languages was shared in the du Pont household. On occasion, playing with both English and French introduces some comical ambiguity: when Tat feels "rheumatic" it is deliberately unclear whether she is bothered by rheumatism or a cold. The use of French in no way hampers general comprehension of the sketches. Charlotte's mammoth bandbox and the puzzled look of the Philadelphia coachman convey the situation without the comic irony of the French title's "petite boîte." And the clumsiness of Starecatus jumping rope does not require the assistance of the title "l' Ecole des Graces" to provoke a smile.

Since the carics were not intended for the uninitiated, they required a minimum of explanation, and for a twentieth-century audience Sophie's letters and diaries provide whatever decoding is needed. They identify subjects like Sir Sprol. And they explain incidents like the encounter with the Quaker gentleman. They also confirm Sophie's natural linguistic ability.

Often in letters to Henry, verbal carics are created—dramatizing the ongoing feud between the carpenters and the painters at Eleutherian Mills (described as the battle between the Knights of the Saw and those of the

Brush) or the arrival of Henry Clay in Wilmington (his steamboat was greeted by "pyramids" of people along the water's edge). Sophie's expressive imagery shows both the richness of two languages and her own originality, as when she speaks of "a mind as *Brumous* as the weather" or of Cousin Frank "gallanting" visitors through the powder yards, but her mastery of language also clearly reflects the period and place of her writing.

Given Sophie's steady reading habits and her familiarity with the Philadelphia literary scene, her prompt adoption of the newest expressions of the day is not surprising. Her use of phrases like "ludicrous phyzes" (funny faces), deer taking "legbail" (making a quick getaway), and "horrific and griffon" errors is worthy of the callithumpian vocabulary appropriate to the Philadelphia of the late 1820s. The fact that "horrifics" became synonymous with "bonnets" on the Brandywine as well as in the city offers tangible proof of the prevalence of the Philadelphia mode, both material and linguistic.

Yet the issues of the day are strangely absent from Sophie's carics. Papa brought home political cartoons, the Smiths and the Bidermanns shared caricatures on such topics as stagecoach rides, and Aunt Josephine and Evelina both passed along satirical drawings of the latest fashions from Europe. Sophie enjoyed them all, and she wrote about them in her letters. Her carics, though, represent her spontaneous response to her immediate surroundings. They spring from her innate sense of humor, coupled with an unusual ability to extract the essence of an incident from its routine context. Because they present sly commentary on the everyday, the ordinary happening, they also depict the trappings of daily life in Sophie's world.

The frequent appearance and many uses of fireplace tongs, chamber pots, and candlesticks are immediately striking in the carics. Various surfaces encumbered with thread, scissors, combs, ribbons, dishes, jars, and sundry articles of clothing indicate the informal ambience. Bedroom scenes reveal all one could want to know about nightdress—from slippers to caps, from bandeaux to sleep tunics—and about bed hangings, bolsters, and dust ruffles. The clutter in the carics emphasizes the general shortage of storage space at Eleutherian Mills, despite the crudely styled tiered hanging shelves, deep and well-filled windowsills, and multitude of bandboxes that supplement the usual bureaus, presses, and armoires.

The rooms are surprising not for their adornment but for their lack of it. There are no bell ropes to summon servants, no richness of trim on window hangings, and but few fashionable turnings on the furniture.

Were it not for the careful drawing of fishbones on a dinner platter, the design of a flagstone floor, the fringe on a hearth rug, it might be judged that the artist dismissed detail as unimportant, or intentionally left her carics unfinished. But attention to such details shows that Sophie's sketches are an honest, forthright portrayal of what she observed.

The simplicity of living at Eleutherian Mills, so strikingly conveyed through Sophie's carics, probably stems from a number of factors. During the decade of her sketches, Papa's establishment was still deeply indebted, and strict economy was important to the household operations. While the du Ponts certainly were acquainted with the high style of the turn of the century in France and were comfortable in the most cosmopolitan settings in America, they were not among the extremely wealthy families in the country. In fact they lagged far behind their planter friends in the South, as well as their merchant friends in Philadelphia and New York. The only suggestions of wealth in their Brandywine home were the extensive family library and family portraits, most of them brought from France.

Considering her parents' dislike of affectation, it follows that lavish ornamentation should be absent from Eleutherian Mills. The du Ponts were comfortable in the semi-isolated rural setting of their home in America, for, like Bois-des-Fossés, their home in France, it was far removed from "society." Their utilization of local labor in building on the Brandywine, their dependence on immigrant help, mostly Irish within the home, and their desire to blend into the modest Quaker neighborhood to which they had moved, all contributed to the unostentatiousness of the life-style they adopted.

Plain furnishings are matched by a lack of lavish adornment in dress. Rarely does Sophie target dress per se in her carics. When she does, it is to mock extremes and uniformity. The inappropriate appearance of high-style Philadelphia faddism in the rustic Brandywine environs, the mania for Scotch plaid cloaks, and the exaggerated sleeves and shoulder patterns of the early 1830s rouse her to satire. For simplicity rules the dress of the du Pont ladies just as it does their household. Except for sleeve puffs, there is remarkable purity of style in both the formal and the wedding attire that Sophie drew: embellishment derived from the flowers, ribbons, combs, and extra twists in coiffure rather than from laces, ruffles, or furbelows in the ladies' dresses.

Conforming with the du Pont taste for unpretentious living, the household was organized country-style. Sophie's caric of the family at dinner shows that meals were ordinarily served "à l'Américain" and not in

1— window looking up the creek,
with view of cottage etc
2— window looking out on piazza,
towards the creek & powder yard
my little white table with my desk on it —
I reading, my book on the stand Alexis made me

Everything here is perfectly lovely, I cannot weary of looking from
my window on the thousand varied hues of the young leaves, & the
dog wood & sassafras blossoms amidst them — I am once more
located in my own quiet nook, Castle Blue —

[S to H, 30 April 1833]

courses as in France. The midday meal was the main one; a very light supper was served at nightfall. Servants did not wear uniforms, and most did not live in. Family pets were part of a lively decor. Indoor activity was generated by imagination or by tasks required for the powder yards or the household. These elements of daily life were common among rural residents and not unique to Eleutherian Mills, a fact that bestows on Sophie's carics an unexpected universality.

On a more intimate level, the carics calendar the years of Sophie du Pont's growing up. Through them she created for herself a special place within her family and circle of friends. Her status secure, she could more easily relinquish the carefree pursuits of her childhood and assume the obligations of womanhood. Sophie herself knew when the time had come. Adopting the decorous demeanor of a young matron of her era, when she married, in 1833, she laid her sketchbook away. Three years later, recounting to her sister-in-law Meta the comedy of a visit from John Phillips that involved his being mistakenly ushered into her boudoir by a flustered maid, she declared:

Whether he beheld me or not, I can't say; if he did he saw the personification of dismay undressed! . . . Since I've recovered from the first agony of horror, I have had a good laugh at the scene, & were I younger would send you & Nora a caric of it— [S to M, 15 November 1836]

Fashionable style of proceeding to pay New Year's visits—

"*Ah migh you pull me down*"
"*Oh you go so fast I cant keep up*"
"*I'm slipping*"
"*Oh! they'll all fall on me! &c   &c   &c*"

[V°]   *January 3ᵈ 1832. Tuesday afternoon—*
M A Lammot—
E Du Pont—
M E Du Pont—
C B Cazenove—
S M Du Pont

On Tuesday we all went over to pay a new year's visit to the overcreekers. . . .
We had a fine scrambling time of it thro' the snow & over the ice—

[S to H, 6 January 1831]

INHABS

*T*he principals in the world of Sophie's carics—the "inhabs," as she called them—were the loved ones of her "heart's home." She deftly but affectionately mocked their eccentricities as she recorded the seasonal doings of the occupants of Eleutherian Mills. When the table tops were strewn with "paste board sheets, coloured papers, and paste cups," New Year's was at hand. Sophie gaily followed the family pattern of fabricating gifts to be exchanged on the first day of the year. A specially covered box for treasures or mineral specimens, an embroidered collar, a watch case, a pincushion, or a tinted map—whatever the gift, it invariably took hours or even weeks of secret labor.

As soon as December arrives . . . all intercourse among the ladies seems to be stopped, all sociability banished, the best friends behave apparently as if they were bitter enemies. . . . ["The Tancopanican Chronicle," 15 January 1825]

Beginning the year together was a French custom the du Ponts had kept after they settled on the Brandywine. The entire family, inhabs and overcreekers, gathered annually for dinner the first day of January. For Sophie, the first celebrations after Mama's death were particularly heartrending. Her presents on January 1, 1830, included a mousetrap from Brother, mittens from Pol, a portfolio for her books of extracts from Evelina, and, from Victorine, a ring containing locks of Mama's hair.

I cannot tell you how I felt when I looked on her fair hair and thought of her whom we always gathered round on a New Year's morning! And you, too, my dear young brothers, when I looked around in vain for your faces, my heart felt sick and heavy and I may say it was to me the saddest New Year's day I ever spent. [S to H, 4 January 1830]

Revelry was the more usual tenor of Sophie's home life. The most trivial incident triggered merriment—and caricature. Though Mama was drawn but once, and Papa never, life at Eleutherian Mills hinged on their needs and wishes. When Papa longed for music at the end of an exhausting day, youthful voices happily serenaded him. Even sister Victorine, mistress of the house after Mama's health declined, deferred to Papa's wishes. When Vic shopped for wallpaper in Philadelphia before Sophie's wedding, Eleuthera reported conscientiously that Papa detested papered rooms: "You ought not to do it without consulting him—" In Vic's defense, Brother

Bidermann praised papered walls, after which Papa pronounced: "Eh bien, si elle est determinée à en mettre un [papier], il faut que je l'achète, car elle n' a point de goût!!!" Indeed, the choice of pattern was Papa's.

Papa was sensitive to the needs of the young people. His spontaneity added to the joy of Sophie's family life. When the winter proved exceptionally snowy, he surprised the family with a sleigh. At the breakfast table one morning, he invited Sophie and her sisters to spend a day at Brandywine Springs, just for the fun of a summertime excursion. While Sophie felt reluctant to venture far from home, she acquiesced for Papa:

> *I took a tremendously long ride (for me) on Saturday–Papa & I left here at half past 7 in the morning & rode 15 miles to Cooch's bridge, to see General Cooch's thrashing machine, which Papa wished to see; we returned by way of Wilmton, which made 17 long miles, in all 32! You will ask what possessed me to go? I did not wish it, but Papa was very anxious to take one of us, & as Tat was not very well, I had to–* [S to H, 21 July 1829]

Finding access to a telescope in New York while on a trip to New Haven, Papa routed the ladies out of their hotel to peer at the moon:

> *After supper we were so tired that we would gladly have retired to bed, but Papa insisted on our going to view the moon thro' a telescope–Notwithstanding my partiality for the orb I went very reluctantly, and lo! when we got there! The telescope man had gone to bed, so that our <u>lunatic excursion proved fruitless</u>.*
>
> [S to H, 11 September 1829]

On that same trip north, Sophie, Vic, and Papa were accompanied by brother-in-law Antoine Bidermann. "Brother," who first came to the Brandywine from France to assess his father's investment in the du Pont gunpowder works, quickly felt at home in this household where his native language prevailed. He soon joined the company, and the family as well. Married to Evelina, the second du Pont daughter, he lived at Eleutherian Mills until after their only child, James, was born. The "Son & Heir," just a year younger than his Uncle Alexis, delighted his aunts by dancing cotillions with them and showing off his first masculine attire, his roundabouts. He was his uncle's built-in companion and a well-loved classmate through school. When Brother traveled on business, young James and his mother stayed at Eleutherian Mills—especially after Evelina seriously injured her foot and had to have it encased in a wooden cast for almost a year.

The son and heir—

We spent last Evening at Bidermanns'—with the assistance of Alexis and James we contrived to make up a cotillon, you would have been amused to see those two boys capering about; James is just promoted to the dignity of round abouts and is not a little proud of his new attire.

[V to SFDP, 26 December 1824]

The lady Barcattus entree at a teaparty— June 9th Friday eve 1826—

Yesterday Barcatus attacked me, and begged me to go and spend a day with his lady, for she is so lonesome. . . . we paid her a visit on Sunday— Her head was full of the fashions she could talk of nothing else, and it was too amusing to hear her—She has bought herself a plaid silk dress of all the colors in the rainbow—It is to be made full all round and fashionable to a degree—I long to see her appear in it— [S to E, 9 October 1826]

Sophie always felt closest to her second sister because they were so much alike—introspective and shy among strangers. Evelina had strong literary tastes, wrote poetry, and enjoyed the Spanish language, just as Sophie did. Their similarity of nature was well noted in the family. Sophie's retiring manners on board the steamboat to New Haven prompted Brother to exclaim, "It's Lina . . . . Just like Lina."

So that Evelina could get outside and move about the neighborhood despite the cast on her foot, Brother purchased a gentle donkey, Annette. Sophie, who injured her knee in 1826, rode Annette from time to time and, when able, joined the entourage promenading with the donkey. Their local adventures were legion:

> *The other day Brother, Lina, James & Eleuthera went to look for some flowers about 2 miles from here—Lina was in the lane with Brother while Tat & James were gathering flowers—(she was on Annette) two old quakers came up in a gig, stopped, & began admiring Annette—at last they asked Lina & brother, if they were travelling "for a show"!* [S to H, 22 May 1830]

A "show" indeed was the arrival of newlyweds on the Brandywine on a sunny autumn Saturday in 1824. A welcoming arch of greenery, cannon salutes, fireworks, and dancing greeted Margaretta Lammot and her bridegroom, Alfred, Sophie's eldest brother, as they moved into Eleutherian Mills to await the building of their new home overlooking the creek. The bride fit into the casual country life with ease, and she allied herself with her sisters-in-law in their escapades. After all, Alfred was a well-known practical joker. He was famous for tampering with any sewing basket he could find; after a quick visit, the young ladies knew just where to look for anything that seemed misplaced, including the candle snuffer. But he was thoughtful of his younger sisters and brothers—ever ready to offer a sleigh ride, a choice mineral specimen, or a puppy. They were not always pleased with his choice of pets; his annoying peacocks seemed to bely his extreme distaste for anything related to luxury. For Alfred was so set on simplicity that he had neither curtains at his windows nor rugs on his floors. Overcreeker cousin Julia remarked that she could look across toward Alfred's new house and almost see him perched like an eagle on his rock. But his sisters thoroughly appreciated the fact that he and Brother both readily permitted fires in the stoves and fireplaces of their homes on a cool day in June or September. At Eleutherian Mills, Mama's French frugality dictated endurance of any chill between mid-April and mid-October.

April 16th 1832
Monday morning—

Did I ever tell you that Alfred has a female Greyhound in addition to Bevis? She is smaller, more delicately formed &
a great deal prettier than him—They call her Flora [S to H, 8 August 1832]

Victorine scrupulously followed Mama's wishes in managing the household. As the eldest, she taught the younger children until they were ready to go away to school. And she served as a role model for her sisters. To young Sophie she represented authority as well as near perfection, and she was therefore a ready target for teenage rebellion. Sophie was deeply hurt when Vic called her a "little goose" or seemed to show the least

Scene 7th A rainy evening—   *1st*   *Vic in a drawling tone "Oh I'm too sleepy aah ho ho*
                                  2d   *Tat—reading old de Genlis. "J'ai un mauvais rheum!!"*
                                         I am very rheumatic ha ha ha—
                                    3   *Soph drawing the annexed, and laughing*

partiality to sister Eleuthera. Intellectually and temperamentally Vic and Tat were highly compatible. Sophie did not simply imagine their closeness, nor could she always control the jealous twinges that assailed her:

Now Eleu is away, I am so constantly with Vic—And 'tis best for me, in some respects—I have not so much op^ty perhaps for reflection, I have less too, for evil thoughts & vain regrets. When Eleu is at home, she & Vic being every thing to each other, I am oftentimes but a super-numerary 3^d person, that is, I am not particularly called upon to exert me to entertain either—when they are conversing &c &c. . . . Now I must read, & talk with Vic—I feel myself of use & comfort to some being at least . . . . [DIARY, 21 February 1833]

Sophie deeply admired Eleuthera, whom she characterized as the "life and sunshine" of their home. Tat was so quick, so vigorous, so like Vic in accomplishment. Recognizing her sister's high energy level, Sophie described her sitting "by the fire, a book open on her knee, while her foot, gracefully waved in measured motion, betokens the activity of her character." But in her carics, Sophie could not resist slyly putting into Tat's mouth the words "Ha . . . Ha . . . Ha." And in her usual self-deprecating manner, she described herself:

Sophie . . . we will commence with her, being the youngest & least important—has nothing remarkable about her— is usually made a great deal too much of at home—and is a perfect insignificant everywhere else—She is sitting by the table, her desk open before her—& is drawing something, from the grin on her countenance it is easy to perceive it is a caricature— [OUR PARLOUR, 2 March 1830]

Perhaps it consoled Sophie to be to her younger brothers, especially Henry, what Vic was to her.

I thought of other Maydays; long past, when you and I were little children—of our walks, and our plays—our bowers, mudhouses, and forts, and the little fleet of boats we used to sail upon the pond—I could not help feeling sad when I thought of how we were changed—we, that once played together, walked together, studied our little lessons in partnership— [S to H, 2 May 1828]

Her correspondence with Henry was unflagging—at once chatty and preachy. She chided him for his quick temper, praised his accomplishments, prayed for his immortal soul—all in relaying in detail the news of the Brandywine Valley. She wrote less frequently to Alexis, for he was closer to home, at Mr. Bullock's school in

Wilmington. But with all her heart Sophie welcomed Lil's visits and vacations. Then his antics and his mischief thoroughly enlivened the household. And she championed his bringing classmates to share the wonders of the countryside after dismal weeks of classwork.

Scene 1ˢᵗ The Bed chamber

1   *Save my pantoufles. save my pantoufles*

2   *ha ha. ha. ha.*

3   *You little goose, What did you do that for?*

Scene 7ᵗʰ

1   *Vic– O! I never was so frightened in my life.*
        feel how my heart beats

2   *Meta O. Sister!*

3   *Eleu–Ha ha–*

Boudoirizing–Sentimentality of Hipopotamus

Mrs Waterman returned here today from New York. She looks about the same as ever, but (although she was fond enough of talking before she went) yet now she has so much to say that I expect a dreadful sore Throat and tongue will be the consequence. [S to H, 16 June 1828]

Sir S–exclaiming with a yawn (addressing the stove)
Thou art the first thought of my awaking
& my last at night!–

Uncle Charles is recovering from his attack of the influenza & passes
all the time between poking the grates & punching the stoves–
[S to H, 29 December 1831]

Mama's younger brother, Charles Dalmas, who was Sophie's mentor in the field of caricature, was himself a very tempting subject. Dubbed "Sir Sprol," he tended to walk on tiptoe and was wont to be overly critical. "Uncle" did battle with sister Vic over how much water the garden should get, worried and fretted over all the residents and their problems, and unfailingly took care of the stoves, swings, mousetraps, and any leftover cheese in the pantry. When Papa hired a new gardener, Sophie wrote prophetically,

I expect he and Sir Sprol will have many a fight–at least Sir S. will be furious, for you know how unhappy his temper is, that he always finds fault with every one and every thing, sure way of making himself unhappy–
[S to H, 11 February 1832]

During the day, Sir Sprol shared the office with Stephens, a general factotum, and Augustus Belin, Papa's accountant. Reporting on the trio, Sophie wrote,

The officers continue as they always have done–Mr Belin writing away, Stephens smoking & reading the papers, & Uncle Charles perambulating the house on tiptoe. [S to H, 19 December 1829]

Two months later she verified the pattern in another letter to Henry:

Mr. Belin and Stephens continue to occupy the office. The former is as good, the latter as lazy as ever. Uncle is still the same wandering genius, now in the garden, then in the cellar, & always "sproling." [S to H, 25 February 1830]

While Papa had great respect and appreciation for Mr. Belin's talents, his daughters named him "Barcatus" and were unmerciful in their critiques of his wife, "Lady Barcatus," who, in the simple farming area of the Brandywine, followed the extremes of Philadelphia fashion.

The young ladies relied instead on the good fashion sense of Mrs. Waterman, a widow with several sons who came to sew for Mama when Alexis was an infant and remained with the family for nearly forty years. Sophie teased "Lady Waters" in 1827 when she took two days off to discharge her duties as first bridesmaid for Betsy Green, a former housemaid. Rumors of Lady Waters' own engagement were rampant, apparently because it was unusual for a forty-year-old matron to serve as bridesmaid. Scarcely daunted by the gossip, the talented seamstress continued threading her needles except when it came time for lengthy visits to her sons in New York, Baltimore, and Philadelphia.

A guest of the family sometimes for weeks, sometimes for months was Pierre Didier, who from the early years of the powder business had served as general physician to the du Ponts and to their employees in the mills on both sides of the creek. As he aged and gradually gave up his practice, the craggy-featured widower divided his time between his house in Wilmington and Eleutherian Mills. The du Pont children privately criticized the repetitive storytelling and gluttonous table manners of "Esculapius," but they respected his medical status. By any standards, his qualifications as a practitioner were startling. With almost no formal education, he wrote his prescriptions phonetically in mixed French and English. He had mastered surgical procedures as an apprentice on the battlefield during the Seven Years' War; he had learned midwifery on the job in the French Caribbean colonies; and he had gained expertise in pharmacology in the course of his sixty years of practice. His preference for homeopathic remedies endeared him to the du Pont household, and he was pleased to pass along his knowledge of herbs, plants, and dosages to Victorine, who helped nurse him during the last years of his life.

These then were the inhabs, the cast of characters in Sophie's earliest drawings. As she matured and the world unfolded before her, new friends and acquaintances joined these early subjects of her carics.

STARECATUS

*T*he first hours of daylight were ideal, Sophie found, for self-imposed intellectual regimens, like her efforts to learn Spanish. The time before breakfast offered her the complete privacy she needed to teach herself her favorite language:

> *Though I could make out to read it, I can no more write in Spanish, than a Hyena. But perhaps, by the time you*
> *know enough to write it, I shall too . . . . I dont like to let any of the family know I continue my attempts, for two*
> *reasons—First, because, as they think it quite impossible I should teach myself anything, they consider it as time*
> *lost—2ᵈ, because as it is very possible I may never attain but a slight knowledge of the language, and that very*
> *slowly . . . I do not wish any but my most intimate friends to know anything about it.* [S to H, 11 June 1827]

But a hideaway corner was not always easy for Sophie to find in the bustling du Pont household. It became almost impossible in 1824 after Papa hired a new chemist, Frenchman Jean Delages, and offered him lodging with the family. Delages, who also took his meals with the du Ponts, was installed in the attic bedroom that was

[*Vᵒ*]

1ˢᵗ   *Vic, all surprise and consternation on entering*
          Starecatus' room and finding him in bed—
2ᵈ   *Starecatus, kicking like all the world.*

Uncle Charles is not very well, and never comes to meals—so
that I thought I should be left tete a tete with Starecatus but
fortunately for me, (unfortunately perhaps for himself) he has
gone on an excursion to the red sea, which you know he never
crosses a sec; I expect he will arrive here dead drunk by way of
rendering himself more agreable.

[S to H, 3 December 1829]

L'Ecole des Graces

[V°]

1   *Starecatus Jumping the rope*

2   *Sophy turning away roaring–*

3-4   *Clem and Lil in admiration!*

reencountre of the President and Starecatus

Last night about midnight Starecatus returned home in about the same situation as he was on a certain Saturday night which you may remember. He fell against the stove in the entry, and the tin plates fell down with a resounding noise, which awoke the whole household; some thought it was firing a pistol, others that it was some one breaking in the house–in short every one was frightened to death–Soon however we heard him come tumbling up stairs, and easily guessed the cause of the uproar. Dont write any thing about this adventure in your letters, as Papa sees them and perhaps he would be vexed that I told it to you. . . . [S to H, 26 March 1827]

Scene 3ᵈ

The consequences of getting up late—
(i.e) a tête a tête with Starecatus—
1ˢᵗ Starecatus—2ᵈ Tat—(both mute)

Sophie's Castle Blue, or her "azure tenement"—her refuge from family scrutiny. That particular room was dear to her brothers and sisters too. There they had set up their "baby house," where Sophie and Alexis had tea parties and arranged candlelight balls for dolls Clara and Lady Editha. And there the children had established their prized Cabinet of Curiosities.

Among the curiosities were Henry's cherished collection of minerals, Alexis' Indian darts, and Sophie's mounted insect specimens, assembled for the Brandywine Entomological Society. Added to these curios were memorabilia like Henry's antique pistols and Lafayette's shoestrings (salvaged by Sophie following the Marquis's visit to Eleutherian Mills). The collections were proudly displayed on special occasions, sometimes with fanciful tales:

> *One Saturday while we were away, Ferdinand [Meta's brother] & Mʳ John Phillips came over. . . . Mʳ Phillips expressed a wish to see some of my insects (for when I was at Lenni I had promised him to show them to him)— Eleuthera went up & brought down several boxes, which he admired greatly. When she went to take them up, Ferd offered to aid her, she accepted–. . . he was perfectly charmed with all the curiosities, which Tat began instantly to display–She first showed him "King Dagoberts spurs," & then pointing to your pistols, assured him they were very antique & valuable <u>having belonged</u> to <u>Francis the 1st!</u> . . . Is she not mischievous!* [S to H, 13 May 1830]

Access to the curios was out of the question while Delages was in residence, a circumstance in itself guaranteed to jeopardize his popularity. Even though he was busy in his small laboratory at the refinery during the day, his privacy had to be respected, and Sophie was driven to practice her Spanish and exercise her literary skills wherever she found a vacant corner downstairs.

Sophie detested the new chemist, whom she dubbed Starecatus because of his fierce, penetrating glance. She remarked on his strong resemblance to simians, and vice versa:

Stephens had a pet monkey some days ago, which he brought here to show us—It was a horrible looking animal,— At least to me, as I have a great dislike to monkeys, which was heightened by the resemblance this one bore to Starecatus. It greatly amused all the rest of the family, particularly little Vic. Stephens however has given it away, because it "skeered" his Henry— [S to H, 19 January 1828]

She expressed her resentment by caricaturing the chemist in humiliating situations; occasions were not hard to find. An opinionated, garrulous know-it-all, Delages before long earned the disdain of all the younger du Ponts:

Starecatus among his <u>news</u> gave us an account of Mr. Whales ball and described it as given by a pension de jeunes demoiselles to Mr Valloux' cadets, whose uniform he likewise described as if no one had ever seen it but him! How long he might have gone on talking of the ball I know not for Vic stopped him short by informing him <u>you</u> were there. At which he only said Ah! Ah! & was mute but began immediately to another subject— [E to S, 5 March 1828]

His quick expression of his thoughts might serve well in after-dinner discussions with Sprol or Doctorus, but the young people all too rapidly discerned that Delages often spoke from ignorance. He could not tell when cider was sour, but was glad to represent himself as an expert. To the amusement of the household Delages thought himself an expert at jumping rope. He even presented himself as an expert on the weather.

Starecatus has predicted clearing today, but I fear he will be a false prophet as usual. [S to H, 18 December 1827]

And, when the forecast proved correct,

The clearing up of the weather this afternoon, was a delightful surprise to us all: for tho' Starecatus had predicted it—you know his prophecies share the fate of those of Cassandra. [S to E, 3 May 1828]

For Delages himself, life on the Brandywine was dull in comparison with the excitement of Paris. He therefore sought solace in occasional prolonged absences from his post.

Starecatus has "adopted invisibility." He has been gone on one of his frolics since a week. [S to H, 12 January 1827]

1st   Sophie, by <u>chance</u>, throwing a handful of old pears on Starecatus.

I have been amusing myself this afternoon firing at a mark—nay, do not start, my <u>weapons</u> were <u>rotten pears</u>, and the big oak my mark—but I can't say I was as successful in the aim as the Cadets we saw firing across the river. [s to h, 1829?]

Several months later, with profound feeling, Sophie reported:

> *Starecatus has disappeared again; he has been gone nearly two weeks—lil and I are much in hopes he will never return, and that we will thus be rid of the only living animal in our museum—Nothing could delight me more as we then would have all his room to ourselves.* [s to h, 24 April 1827]

But her wish was not to be granted. Alas, Starecatus had merely embarked on another of his periodic "treks to the red sea," from which he would drag home hung over and penitent. At such times Sophie's only consolation was that he required some days more for full recovery:

> *Papa and I have been tête à tête at every meal but dinner since you went and I expect I shall be perfectly alone tomorrow, Starecatus being still imersed in the red sea. But solitude is better than <u>such</u> company as <u>his</u>, I am sure you will own—* [s to v, 4 December 1827]

Jubilation reigned when sister Eleuthera announced to Sophie, then visiting in Philadelphia,

> *Joyful news have I to communicate. We are delivered from the annoyance of Starecatus! He went to Papa in Ph^a & gave him up all the keys of the Laboratory etc & requested his clothes should be sent up to him tomorrow—dont be too much <u>amazed</u> if he should bow to you as you are parading Chesnut St. some day.* [e to s, February 1828]

[*V°*]

Starecatus, engaged in a conflict with the dogs—

[*V°*]

Starecatus's gallant exploit—
(ie) putting Azor to flight
with no other weapon but the broomstick—

Azore begins to make great use of his horns—Mr. Brilliant (a frenchman who works in the refinery,) plagueing him with Stephens, through the bars of the gate—a little after dinner Mr Delages went to go down and Brilliant accompanied him Azore let Mr Delages pass but he flew at Brilliant and threw him down—Stephens seized him by the horns and pulled him away—Brilliant got up again, but no sooner was Azore loose than he attacked him again, pushed him over the wall in front of the piazza and jumped over after him—Alex arrived and gave Azore a knock on the head with a stick of wood which hurt him a good deal—they at length succeeded in getting Brilliant away—ever since this the men are so much afraid of Azore that they will not pass thro' the park though he is gentle as ever with us—

[S to H, 17 November 1824]

Eventually Dr. Didier supplied the explanation of the chemist's absence from his post at Eleutherian Mills:

> *He left here 6 weeks ago on one of his accustomed peregrinations & we heard nothing of him for four weeks. The Doctor then told us that he was in town & had paid him two visits at one of which he was completely <u>qualified</u>. Doctor scolded him & advised him to come home: he excused himself by saying "Que voulez vous! je m'ennuie chez Mr. Dupont. Il n'y a pas de société!"–Last week when Papa was in Ph^a he went to Mr Gurney Smith's counting house to speak to Papa. . . . I hope we are fairly rid of the disagreable creature, who I am sure cannot be more tired of our <u>societé</u> than we are of his.* [E to Ev, 25 February 1828]

Sophie's elation was short-lived. About a week later she wrote to Evelina:

> *The latest news here, and the worse, is that Starecatus is actually returned. We saw him enter the yard at dusk so there is an end to hope.* [S to Ev, 6 March 1828]

And two weeks later:

> *I have drawn a good many caricatures since you went, but not <u>lately</u>, as I was too furious at Starecatus' return. I had such a false joy about his going away.* [S to Ev, 20 March 1828]

Delages's final date of departure from the Brandywine is uncertain, although his replacement (another Frenchman, Lecarpentier) was at work in late summer the next year, 1829. Rather than live at Eleutherian Mills, Lecarpentier boarded with a neighboring farmer. It was mid-May 1830 before the imprint of Starecatus was at last erased from the attic.

> *On Monday Alexis & I removed <u>all</u> the things out of Delages room carefully into the garrets, which we locked–Sister then had our room washed, scrubbed & whitewashed–On Tuesday lil and I fixed every thing in again, first dusting & wiping all with great care–Our Attic room looks like a palace now, & we are going to give a coat of white paint to the window, which will be another improvement. Alexis has painted several of my insect boxes white–For I found that none of my insects kept so well as my small phalenas do, in the box you made & painted for me–*
>
> [S to H, 13 May 1830]

CHAMBERS AND CHAMBER POTS

*T*o be alone at Eleutherian Mills was a rarity. Sophie reported only one instance when she was

quite alone, the girls being stormbound at the Gilpins. The whole house was dark as midnight, all the shutters being closed, except when the vivid flashes of lightning streamed through the crevices. The wind raged without with great violence, the rain poured down in torrents, and the thunder rolling above added to this awful scene. I must confess as I walked through the dark entries and tenantless chambers, to see that all was secure, I felt I was indeed <u>completely alone in my father's house!</u> [S to H, 25 June 1829]

As a rule, Eleutherian Mills overflowed with spirited occupants, who—unlike Starecatus—were made to feel welcome. A fire kindled in a bedchamber on a chilly morning, a quick, quiet rearrangement of sleeping quarters, a joyful greeting à la française, a fresh bouquet from the garden—these and other gestures of hospitality made guests eagerly anticipate their trips to the Brandywine.

Overnight guests often came to see Papa on business, or to visit one or more of the young du Ponts. Especially during the summer months, simple country living was a magnet to city folk. Eleutherian Mills was at an ideal excursion distance from Wilmington, from Philadelphia (as long as the steamboats were running), and from Brandywine Springs, popular area spa of the day. The gardens, the deer park, and the unfailing hospitality of the du Pont house made it an attractive destination; the powder mill alongside gave it particular appeal for the gentlemen. Sometimes late-afternoon visitors had to be invited to spend the night.

In the afternoon, while I was sitting at work in Mama's room two young grampuses from Berlin arrived to see the mills. Papa went down to them, and Mama and <u>I</u> were terrified least they should stay to sleep–but fortunately they soon decamped. [S to H, 4 December 1827]

When cholera was rampant in Philadelphia, the entire Richard Smith family sought refuge with their friends on the Brandywine, and the Gurney Smith children from next door came too:

M^r *& M*^{rs} *Richard Smith are here with Clem, Harriet & Horace–And we still have Joanna, Maria, Frank & Decatur–As you may suppose Joan's very anxious about her father & Mother & brothers. . . . we are crowded as* *full as the house can stow. . . . M^r & Mrs Smith talk of leaving us on Friday or Saturday, as Mr R^d Smiths business will recall him—Till then I am going to stay at Meta's, our house not affording me room —*

[S to H, 8 August 1832]

There were instances in which it was unclear under whose auspices guests were invited.

This afternoon just after I had written to you the two little Porters arrived here from Bullocks [school] to stay till Monday—We did not expect them, but I suppose Papa asked them. . . . Theodoric the eldest, I suppose is about 11 or 12, Hamilton about 8 or 9. . . . They are now roaming about, I don't know where but 'tis the hardest thing in the world to entertain boys— [S to H, 17 April 1830]

In "The Tancopanican Chronicle" there is a more fanciful account:

Theodoric king of the ostrogoths & his royal brother came to our surprise to remain till Monday. Their visit proved a perfect nuisance & entirely discomposed Sister who did not recover from the effects of their misdemeanors for several days—

Pernicious effects of reeding tails

Reeding tails (a play on words, referring to the long, accordion-pleated, or "reeded," skirt worn by the young lady).

Occasionally a chance acquaintance took advantage of du Pont hospitality.

We were surprised to see arrive in our dearborne, an old gentleman who announced himself as Mr. Alexander of Baltimore, & without further ceremony, established himself here for the night! Papa had no recollection of him at first but at last remembered having been introduced to him many years ago in Baltimore—Oh my dear, such an oddity!. . . Since he is gone we have found he is a little demented, not to say entirely cracked. He came here to tell about a wonderful secret he had discovered for cleaning wool for manufacturers, which was, to wash it with <u>eggs</u>! . . . only think the thousand eggs it would take! He departed yesterday afternoon. . . . We were delighted that Mr. R. S. persuaded him to go off— [S to H, 1 5 August 1 8 3 1]

It was so difficult to maintain a clear picture of room occupancy around the clock from one day to the next that the late-afternoon distribution of chamber pots fresh from their daily airing could be a disturbing adventure. The distributor had to be careful not to burst into a room where one of Papa's agents, wearied by an excessively long journey, might be taking a refreshing nap before or after transacting his business. The chamber pots distributed for nighttime and emergency use were supplanted during the day by the high-windowed

[Vº]

Jane McMullin and Mʳ McEwen
(Jane at twilight bumps in the room
& stops transfixed seeing him on the bed,
when she thought the room empty—)

retiring room, also variously known as Grimgothico, the Mrs. Adams, the Mrs. Jones, and P. Pott's Hall. Inhabs who had been visited by a doctor or doctored by Vic rarely roamed far from the Necessary:

The Dr's medicine had a fine effect: and has caused us much amusement. . . . I sewed furiously but poor Sophie had to fly to <u>P. Pott's hall</u> *so often that she could not settle to anything else.* [E to V, 26 January 1832]

Despite the many comings and goings and despite the frequency of a "posse of visitors," the household held to an established pattern of morning activity. During Mama's lifetime, it revolved around her. Then, after 1828, Victorine's bedroom became the center of activity early each morning. There the young people gathered to brush their teeth, wash up, and assemble for breakfast. The young ladies depended on the services of Mrs. Waterman as they dressed for the day. Scurrying about before the bell signaled breakfast invariably created a clutter of containers, combs, and ribbons on the mantel and every other available surface. And as they headed downstairs for their repast, they left behind a heap of nightcaps, bandeaux, linen tunics, and other articles of nightdress—to be sorted or put away later in the morning.

Hospitality

Last night, (as having so much company, we were somewhat pinched for room) I flung a shawl about me, & ran up to Meta's, to share Mary's apartment—It was ten oclock, & you would have laughed at their surprize on seeing me—Only think what lazy girls she & I were, we did not rouse till Meta <u>incensed</u>, *rushed into our room after 7 oclock to tell us breakfast was ready—* [S to H, 25 June 1830]

A morning scene in Vics room

A Summers day on the Tanco—

The sun has long illum'd the morning skies
When, half by peacocks waken'd, half by flies,
With dreams still floating oer the drowsy sense
And eyes scarce op'd, the toilet we commence—
This task but half perform'd we startled hear
The breakfast bell come thundering on our ear—

By this dire sound to sudden speed impell'd
The ling'ring mists of slumber are dispell'd—
The morning's plain attire is don'd in haste
And round the board by slow degrees we're plac'd
On piles of cakes there hunger spends its rage,
And little converse can the mind engage.

In the very beginning Papa had found the plans for Eleutherian Mills were much "too grand" for his taste, but that was some eight years before Sophie was born. By the time Sophie started drawing her carics, it was not unusual to run out of sleeping space. Sophie did not in the least mind doubling up with Nora or Joan or Clem or Lotta, or even sharing a bed with Ella or Tat. But she preferred keeping some sleeping distance between herself and Vic, who tended to regiment any young ladies who joined her or took possession of her recessed bed. Vic's authoritative presence squelched their merriment, suppressed their high jinks.

Left alone, Sophie frequently captained a lively brigade of young women intent upon bedtime fun. Soon after her twentieth birthday she wrote:

> *I do not feel much older though I have bid adieu to my teens. Ella declared I was grown ten times <u>wilder than before!</u>* [S to H, 28 September 1830]

[*V°*]   *1ˢᵗ*   *Victorine opening the door, and encountering Thomson*
            2ᵈ   *Thomson—Ha! ah! Mrs. Bauduy is undrest!!!!!!!!*

Evening Parade

Charlotte and I are quite in despair; because this morning we had to make a grand movement from our apartment the blue room, to the passage room, which was a vast deal of trouble! when lo! This afternoon who should arrive but Mr. Thomas Haven from Philad^a! So we are obliged once more to shift our quarters, march, with our baggage & accoutrements into Vics room & encamp there. We do not admire the new station at all, as the commander in chief Victorine, is very strict in beating reveille in the morning betimes & also in seeing our lights out by 9 oclock —

[S to H, 13 January 1831]

Ella was in fact the frequent target of mischief, because Sophie discovered she was inordinately fearful. She was disgusted when Lady Bristlebrow behaved badly during a session with Dr. Hudson, the Philadelphia dentist, and thenceforth made her the object of teasing.

> *Oh I can scarce tell what I'm writing Ella is making me roar so with descriptions of her various <u>fights</u> with <u>Corporal</u>*
> *<u>O'Possumtail</u>. Amongst others, do you remember one in the garden, with certain green caterpillars for <u>weapons</u>.*
> *They were <u>most powerful ones</u> against <u>her ladyship</u>; she is a dreadful coward, & I had well nigh <u>terrified</u> her just*
> *now by coming pounding up the stairs with a <u>masculine tread</u>–* [S to H, 6 June 1832]

Only when Ella sought Papa to be her defender did Sophie bring the teasing to a halt, for his intensely stressful business schedule made all his children protective of his rare moments of rest.

> *After our guests were gone, & Pol & Ella were sewing sedately upstairs, I marched by the pantry stairs & knocked*
> *loudly at the door–Pol knew it was me, but Lady Bristlebrow, turning pale, (for she thought me in Pa's room)*
> *exclaimed "whats that! Oh Pol!" Pol, for fun, said in a tone of alarm, "Oh migh, Ella What shall we do!"*
> *instantly lady Bristlebrow flung herself into the duena's arms, & implored her protection– "fly Ella" cried Pol–she*
> *took the hint & rushed into the doctors room dragging the roaring Pol after her; I with that entered Vics room &*

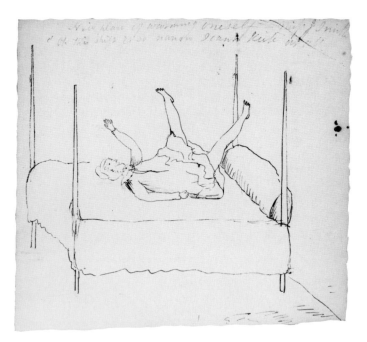

Nice plan of warming oneself–
Miss J Smith   "Oh this shift is so narrow I can't
kick at all!"

taking the hearth brush, after once more knocking at the door between the two rooms, poked the handle of the hearth

brush thro' the door– "Oh wha! wha! whaw! Yeow!" cried Ella, "there is a <u>gun</u>, Pol, I see it" and vowing she'd call

Papa, she rushed toward his room, when Pol & I instantly stopped her, & told her who it was–she was horridly

frightened– [S to H, 22 March 1830]

"You know I always had a *little* mischief in my nature," admitted Sophie to her brother Henry in a letter of

31 July 1829. But occasionally the joking backfired. Once when Sophie and company crept out of the house to

perform a discordant midnight serenade under Nora's window, Sir Sprol locked them out.

[*V°*]

Effects of midnight rambles–(an awful noise)

1 Soph   "Oh my dear! have you knocked down
*   the house?"–*

2 Lotte   (terrified) "Ah migh! I did not stop to
*   pick up the sticks! the doctors candle is*
*   not out!"*

1 Soph   "Hark! I hear Sprol tripping upstairs!"

2 Lotte   "Oh I'm sure I've waken'd the whole
*   house hold–"*

[*V°*]   *A surprize on New Years morning*

*   he– "let me in! Let me in"–*
lady– maintains a dignified silence & makes
*   obstinate resistance. "Let me in I say"–*
Door bursts open–both parties in utter consternation–
"Oh! I beg your pardon,
*   I didnt know 'twas you!! a precipitate retreat–*
*   lady– left squaling–*

January 1ˢᵗ 1834

The other night Joanna, Lil, & I, went up again & serenaded Elenora & Elisa. Lil had that little squeaking fife, you used to excoriate our ears with—Joanna & I had <u>combs</u>. The ladies were all asleep, but the <u>enchanting melody</u> at last dispelled their slumbers, & two white-robed forms appeared at the window—We yelled to them to come down, which Elenora did, & after a short conversation we returned home—when conceive our horror! to find Sprol had locked us out! Lil went round to try & get in at the piazza door, meantime Sprol came and unlocking the front door, threw it open & burst forth in our astonished gaze, clad in nothing but a <u>scant linen tunic!!!</u> fortunately Joan was behind me, & was not so much <u>shocked</u> as I was—"Oh we can get in by ourselves!" cried I to him, retreating precipitately—He took the hint & retired to the office, while we rushed in & flew to admit Lil by the piazza door which he also found locked—we are every night expecting that the girls from Metas will come to <u>serenade us</u>, when they shall have a <u>cool reception</u>, in the shape of a basin full of water I am determined— [S to H, 26 August 1831]

An earlier serenade had been scarcely more successful:

I like amusement, fun, sociability, &c but all to a rational extent. . . . at about ten oclock, Vic packed us all to bed—In going into our ovens of rooms, we were so hot we determined to go to the Pump for water—Accordingly Clem—Pol & I set out When at the pump, "Oh" cried I, "lets run off & serenade Elenora" "O yes!" screamed my companions, & throwing our frocks over our heads away we flew to Metas—where at last after fifty adventures we got under Nora's window. . . . Pol whispered she heard steps slowly descending within the house!—Off we scampered all three in different directions & at last got home—But I never laughed more I think—As we were undressing us, we heard something pelting against our window curtain, we suspected a foe, but hearing nothing more at last concluded 'twas a bat. [S to H, 10 August 1831]

Night noises in the large house only raised the spirits of Sophie and her friends. Sometimes the scratching of rats initiated midnight rambles and adventures; sometimes the wanderings of inhabs provoked action. Tat locked the bedroom door when she heard Sir Sprol "peregrinate furiously" below. But Sir Sprol's nighttime patrols were a protection as well as an annoyance. Papa was frequently away on business, and Uncle felt responsible for the safety of the house.

This morning at about five o'clock Meta was awakened by a slight smell of smoke, she woke Alfred. . . . Alfred went

to his sanctum, & the moment he opened the door, called out "tis my room" & closing it up tight, for twas suffocating

with smoke, & air would but increase the fire, he all the servants & Meta brought up water, which he kept flinging into

the room & then rushing back to put his head out of the window to breathe, so dense was the smoke—The origin of the

fire is traceable to Alfred's carelessness, & ought to be a good warning to all gentlemen, who are very apt to <u>snuff</u>

<u>candles</u> with the first thing they reach—He snuffed his last night with one of his pincers & the snuff dropped in a box of

saw dust & shavings near his lathe—His mind misgave him it might do some harm, so he went back & tramped on it,

till he felt secure it was all out—Yet it is evident the fire originated in that very box! [S to H, 1 December 1832]

When powderman François Jeandel's farmhouse burned, all the inhabs were forcefully reminded of their vulnerability. The alarm sounded through the valley:

We were awakened by the factory bell over the creek ringing violently–We sprang out of bed (That is, Vic & I, who were alone at home) and flew to the window but could see nothing–It was then near 2 oclock–Just then we heard a noise on the piazza, & throwing up the window, beheld uncle in a <u>slight linen tunic</u>, (with no other covering) dancing & kicking about to keep himself warm–"Oh what is the matter!" cried Vic to him–"Eh mais! je n'en sais rien, je suis à me geler ici!" responded he in a despairing tone–At that moment in rushed Mary Green, in her night gown, <u>shrieking</u>–Vic told her to go to Watson and tell him to bring us word what was the matter–Off she ran just as she was. . . . At last Watson came back with the intelligence that the farm house in which François lived, had been burnt to the ground! . . . I assure you we were terribly frightened, for at first we were sure the factory was on fire. [S to H, 1 November 1831]

Factory fires were by no means uncommon.

Mr. Swift informed us that Mʳ John Connelly's factory took fire last Tuesday night, but after some difficulty they succeeded in extinguishing it, with no other loss to the establishment than the cotton & lighter articles in the room– Poor John Connelly, however, met with the most horrible loss in his own personal possessions, the envious flames having actually consumed his–– <u>whiskers!!</u> If you've ever seen the youth, you'll probably remember the luxuriant groves of bristles which vegetate on his visage, & may conceive his mortification at the conflagration–

[S to H, 15 October 1832]

With no fire engines to call on, the fear of fire, especially in the vicinity of the powder mill, was in no way exaggerated. Any container at hand was used to control a fire in its earliest stages. Whether a blaze originated from a clogged chimney, a coal-spitting fireplace, or a carelessly snuffed candle, chamber pots ranked along with pitchers and buckets as means of quenching flames before they engulfed a room or, worse yet, a home. Sophie, when placed with Tat in temporary charge of Eleutherian Mills, reassured Vic:

We will take care that the <u>fires</u> should burn, & the <u>house should not</u>– [S to V, 26 January 1832]

OUR PARLOUR

*S*o important was the parlor at Eleutherian Mills that Sophie was inspired to describe its entire contents in a twelve-page booklet dated March 2, 1830, and titled "Our Parlour: Sketches of winter scenery and amusements," parodying the prosy style of Mrs. Mitford's *Our Village.*

Among the whole range of our apartments, there is none which affords more material for description, than our parlour.—Let us enter it at once—and we will begin the investigation of its contents by the side nearest the door. First then, on the left hand as you enter, there is a corner—occupied by what it is difficult to describe, but which was intended for an elegant workstand. It is tall, slender, & formed partly of mahogany, partly of crimson velvet. Upon it usually rests a large drawing case, half open to the dust & air—this is surmounted by a massy & classic assemblage of volumes, among which the household register "(accountbook)" & the album of the renowned personage, A. Fountain Esqr "(ie, the store book)" shine conspicuous. [S to H, 9 March 1830, quoting from "Our Parlour"]

Prominent among the room's furnishings was the piano. Shipped by packet from Philadelphia, it arrived on the Brandywine without legs, a cause of great consternation until the good news was announced:

The long agony is over! The piano legs are restored . . . these supporters of harmony have at length been discovered in the store of the New Castle Steamboat in Philadelphia. ["The Tancopanican Chronicle," 13 December 1823]

It was Eleuthera who played the piano (she had studied music with Mr. Charles Hupfeld in Philadelphia), but it was Sophie who loved to dance. Her piety conflicted with her passion for dancing, but she persuaded herself that if missionary Harriet Newell had danced on her way to convert the heathens, it must be an acceptable exercise.

On Saturday afternoon, Mary came to our house. . . . Suddenly, Tat went to the piano & began singing a parody of a song which set us all in such high spirits, that when she struck up a waltz, Mary & I dashed away our work & set to dancing. [S to H, 27 January 1831]

Tat was the pianist, but Sprol was resident musician—self-taught fiddler, pianist, and guitarist—and totally French. When Ella requested guitar lessons, he was charmed—and paid her a thousand compliments.

After dinner as we were seated in the parlour, we beheld him enter, an old cracked guitar in one hand & a gamut in the other. Ella instantly rose, I impelled by curiosity, followed. Imagine the group which then presented itself in the centre of our parlour–Sir S. supporting one end of the guitar, Ella the other. The said relic of departed ages had returned disabled of three strings from the wars (with the rats). Sir S. began his instructions, flying about from one thing to another, so Ella could not understand; she was exclaiming, "What must I do? Where must I put my fingers? Is it here? Is it there?" I, standing between the two, with one hand holding up Sir S.'s written instructions, with the other pulling Ella's fingers along the strings into the proper places, & acting as interpreter to Sir S.'s incomprehensible phrases–such a scene! I was almost convulsed with laughter, but durst not give way to it, for fear of enraging the master. In this style we got through the first lesson. Je compte en faire un dessein if I've time.

[S to E, 1 April 1831]

Sophie did sketch Uncle Charles performing as a one-man band: seated at the piano, playing the guitar, beating a small drum with his foot, and smoking a cigar.

With words or with jackstones, spirited parlor games pitted sister against sister, cousin against cousin. And, in 1829, the young Gilpins introduced charades to the Brandywine after a visit to their grandfather in England. Sophie's natural shyness vanished totally in the excitement of playing the new game.

Evening pastimes
Romance and comfort
Tu le veux donc, oh peine extreme   &c &c

We had quite a musical soiree–Duo, Miss V. E. du Pont & Miss E. P. du Pont . . . solo, Mr. Charles Dalmas on the guitar . . . played with violent execution . . . interspersed with comments such as the following, Je vais fricasse cette guitar, car les cordes sont trop durs–poor Ella's instrument! [S to E, 1831]

Studying the graces, a waltzing lesson

[*V°*] 1 *Elenora, waltzing mistress*

          Hold your frock up Soph and let me see your feet There, do it <u>gracefully</u>—

  2^d *Soph "Is that right mistress is that the graceful style*

  3^d *Elisa Oh not half high enough—*

  1st *Elenora "Kick out yr feet more—*

Returned on the horse—found dear Nora here—waltzed a while I am passionately fond of this exercise—but could I for a moment suppose that my partiality for it would <u>ever</u> induce me to attempt it in public, or with a gentleman, I should <u>never try</u> it again—Most religious people so decidedly disapprove of dancing that I often have doubts as to its being an innocent amusement—One thing I am sure is that in cities, waltz parties lead to much evil—but I cannot think the mere dancing with Nora for exercise, is any more improper than running a race down the garden walk, or scrambling over the hills— [DIARY, 9 February 1831]

We had great fun Saturday afternoon, acting charades. . . . We acted impart, (as <u>imp first</u>) Tat dressed up with long paper horns, & tail—but unhappily they all mistook her for Old Nick. <u>part</u> we acted as the separation of two lovers—I was the Lady, Tat in Pa's clothes my lover—the audience were much affected by our evident grief & emotion, as our smothered peals of laughter passed for stifled sobs. We had the greatest amusement, and all frequently exclaimed, "Oh if Henry were only here," or "Oh! how well Corporal could assist us!"

[S to H, 12 December 1829]

For Sophie's twentieth birthday, Mary Gilpin designed and made an unusual present—"a large paper flower with a charade written on each leaf, 'tis pretty and amusing." Charades, games, and theatrics—in French and English—stretched the imaginations and strained the wardrobes of the du Pont household.

The rehearsals are commonly the occasion of most agreable parties. . . . It puts presses, store rooms, sometimes even parlours topsy-turvy. . . . We have a wide choice of plays in the two large libraries on both sides of the creek and if we can enlist in the company that distinguished engineer Alfred V. Dupont Esqʳ and that elegant and ingenious artist Chˢ Dalmas Esqʳ we will not be in want of any thing.

["The Tancopanican Chronicle," 11 October 1823]

Scene 2. Jackstones. the parlour.

1   *ha-ha it is not a miss*

2   *Yes it is. it is. it is—*

3   *Now Alfred was it not a miss*

4   *I dont know love*

Messrs. Editors

Having lately paid a visit to one of the families settled on the Tancopanican, I was much surprized on entering the parlour to find several of the young ladies standing around the table engaged in tossing up marbles; but I was soon informed that this was one of the fashionable amusements this winter; and that Jack stones, which formerly served only as a pastime for idle school girls has now succeeded to chess, battledoor & former favorites. But while my faculties were all deeply absorbed in that most difficult trial of skill—No crackums.—I was suddenly roused by the cries of Sneak, Sneak; and turning round discovered a young couple seated on the floor. "My love, why don't you sneak" said the husband. "Oh my dear, you are fat" answered his spouse.—It was fortunate that I had some knowledge of technical terms and thereby discovered that they were much interested in a game at Marbles!

["The Tancopanican Chronicle," 15 January 1825]

The men of the family got into the spirit of an after-supper performance, costume and all. When Uncle Charles played a major role, Sophie was prompter.

> *They acted Mr. Fothery. . . . brother alias Mr. Fothery was dressed as usual, only that he had a cane—Uncle Charles, Lapierre, was in a blue nankin coat with yellow flannel collar, buttons, and sleeve cuffs—Vic, as Mrs. Dubre with a cap on, and a pair of gloves, a fan and a pocket handkerchief and Eleuthera as young Dub in a pair of white pantaloons and brother's large great coat looked so singular that I can give you no idea of it—I was souffleur and therefore not permitted to look off the book but when Tata entered I looked up for an instant and her appearance made me laugh so immoderately that had they forgotten their part at that moment it would have been impossible for me to do my office.* [S to H, 10 January 1825]

Activity in the parlor was not always so boisterous.

> *We spend day after day, quietly and happily enough, in reading, drawing, sewing, conversation and music.*
>
> [S to H, 12 January 1831]

All the young du Ponts were voracious readers, Sophie's complaint that she could read only "in patches and snatches . . . between the laborious duties of housekeeping" notwithstanding. So that domestic chores might not be interrupted, entire books were read aloud, readers taking turns while listeners cut labels or stitched powder bags for Papa's business, or did mending, quilting, or fine embroidery. Scott's novels were all the rage the instant they appeared in Philadelphia—printed in such haste that Vic's copy of *The Pirate* was missing a few sheets. Cooper's most interesting novel, Sophie thought, was *The Red Rover*, no doubt because Cousin Frank read it aloud and explained the seafaring terms. For the whole of one winter Gibbon's *History of the Decline and Fall of the Roman Empire* was fashionable on both sides of the Brandywine. Uncle Charles read a French edition, while his nieces got through the eight volumes in English only by dint of diligent reading before breakfast. Despite the apparently soporific effects of reading books by the Reverend Charles S. Stewart, at least one of his travel accounts was a great favorite:

> *Charlotte and I were also reading his journal of his residence among the Sandwich Islanders, one of the most interesting & amusing books I ever read.* [S to H, 13 January 1831]

Scene 6th   The pleasures of Society—
1st Vic, 2d Tat, 3d Soph, all reading—
4th Enter Meta "Well upon my word! this is very entertaining!
I wish I had brought my book too!—

Effects of reading Stewart

Effects of reading Stewart

[V°]

Lotta & Soph asleep on the sofa—
Vic dropping asleep & letting the book fall,
yawning out faintly "Some one take it—I'm asleep"
Tat looking up indignantly from her <u>embroidery</u>
"Well thats too bad!"   January 9th 1831

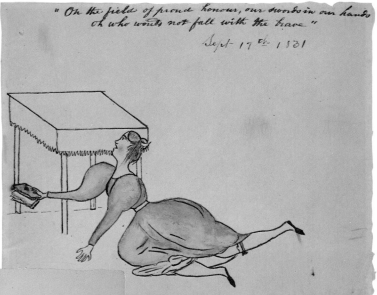

I am Despairing! Oh–Alas–agony–
(She falls fainted against the sofa)–
Aunt Dorothea Page 5th–

"On the field of proud honour, our swords
in our hands
Oh who would not fall with the brave"
Sept 17th 1831

Scene 4th

1   *L-O-R-D. lord-s-h-i-p-hip.–*
2   *No. Ship–Mary.–*
1   *S-H-I-P–ship–Happyship.–*
2   *No its lordship.–*

[*V°*] 1st   Brother Bidermann running off with his wife–

2d   Evelina crying "carry me up, carry me up Oh, ho, Oh!–

3d   Sophy, squaling. "Oh! a poko! a poko Meta, Meta, I have no pocko!–

4th   Victorine– "Oh the blanket!–shall I take it down–No–Yes–
          Oh, I'll have time!"–

5th   Meta– "Down with the blanket fast, fast! Oh the double gilts–
          Old Pomponius himself"–

6th   Niece frightened to death, clinging to Sophy and squaling–

A call from Mr Carroll, the Catholic priest, and a Mr Barry.–Caught our parlor in a dishabille."–
                        ["The Tancopanican Chronicle," 1 April 1830]

The activity of the parlor's inhabs ranged beyond the arts of leisure and domesticity. In this multipurpose room Vic practiced the art of vaccination on siblings and children of the mill workers. When Doctorus was not in residence she also dispensed medical advice.

> *This afternoon as Vic and I were quietly at work in the parlor, "a patient called" & was introduced to the presence of our learned lady Hypocratia—the patient having stated that her face burned, sister pronounced the disease a burning of the face—but what almost upset my gravity was her constantly appealing to me & consulting me about her prescriptions—However, I screwed up my face into the proper expression of importance & dignity as I answered, "yes, certainly, vinegar & water is very cooling"—"True, cream might be refreshing" "yes milk & water is an excellent thing &c &c"... as soon as the patient departed, I requested sister never to mistake me for her apprentis again.* [S to E, 1 April 1831]

By the time Sophie wrote her description, this center of so many activities was a far cry from a proper Victorian parlor. The horsehair sofa had lost its sable sheen and was slipcovered—"robed in full attire of white dimity and occupied by divers dirty pocket handkerchiefs, mittens, shawls, cloaks, workbags, and what not." The cluttered parlor she portrayed was a family room ahead of its time, frequently in such a state of confusion that Papa's unexpected arrival with a business acquaintance sent his daughters scurrying to make the room, and themselves, presentable.

> *On Thursday Pa told us he expected a gentleman from the west of Penn^a ... a Mr Read—I heard this, but concluding it was some ostrogoth never thought of it again particularly as 'twas pouring & we all had concluded he would not come.... Our parlour was in the greatest deshabille I have seen it in since the memorable day of Messrs. Carroll & Co.'s invasion—I was dissecting old frocks, here lay an antiquated sleeve, there a wing estropiée, the body in my hands, the other members parsemant the neighbouring chairs—myself in a brown study over the relics—I was roused by an exclamation in the entry of "How do you do Mr Read." Instinctively I caught up the nearest articles & darted out of the room by one door as Pa and Mr R. pounced in the other. I rejoined Vic... just then something was wanted in the parlour—Vic descended as she was, ses cheveux coiffées à la Méduse, dress to correspond, &c &c She came up, much shocked to have presented herself in this trim before Mr Colin Read whom she had seen at Mrs. Smith's last week. You may suppose I laughed.* [S to E, 26 March 1831]

[V°]

1   Joan! Wha a ha ha tremendous screech & crash–
2   Soph "Oh migh! She'll crush uncle she's thro'
*   the floor!–   July 28ᵗʰ 1832 Monday*

We have yet to examine the reading desk, a perfect original of its
kind–an inclined plane on an upright stick, the whole neatly cov-
ered in azure paper (this is the desk Lil and I made)
   [S to H, 9 March 1830, quoting from "Our Parlour"]

Though Sophie was amused by sister Vic's discomfiture, she did not take lightly the importance of being always presentable for Papa's sake.

I resolved today I'll try & dress always in such a manner that I would be able unblushingly to render the duties of hospitality to any who come under my father's roof. [DIARY, 24 June 1832]

The most careful preparations were no guarantee against surprise when Papa's political friends came calling. One such disconcerting event was Henry Clay's arrival in 1833 with an unexpected suite of campaign followers,

which consisted of the committees from Wilmington & Philadᵃ, & some from Baltimore, & a troop of Vulgarians & oddities of all sorts, drunk & sober. . . . He arrived in Wilmington last Wednesday by the morning boat–The wharves were crowded with spectators, & the woodpiles being covered with men & boys, had, I am told a very fine *appearance from the Boat, resembling pyramids of people. . . . After submitting most graciously to have his paw shaken by all those who desired the honour, he was invited to go out to M*r *Milligans & partake of a cold colation. . . . They all re-mounted & proceeded to our house. As this was merely a* visite d'amitié *from M*r *Clay to Papa, we expected 'twould go off very* genteely *& did not anticipate the quantity & quality of his escort—accordingly we had merely set on the piano three or four waiters of wine & water, a silver basket of Pommes d'Api, one of cake, & a poundcake on the table—My dear they vanished in an instant, like the dew before the sun of the morning! Such a* ravenous *&* odd *set I never beheld! When we saw them coming we took to flight up stairs to contemplate them from the upper windows—But Papa immediately sent up for us; Ella, Victorine, Eleuthera & I descended, & were introduced by him to M*r *Clay. . . . I thought M*r *Clay very homely, but he certainly has a pleasing agreeable face—He staid here some time & we remained in the parlour till we could effect our escape from the crowd.*

[S to H, 2 November 1833]

Scene II The discovery of the Scissors

1   *Not satisfied with one, I've brought home two!!*
2   *Ah ha Ah!!! How could you do such a thing!*

Halloween

1   Eleut– *"Polly, who is that next to Mr Connelly"*

2   Pol–Hugh <u>Smith</u>

(Peering into a good fire on Halloween was said to reveal the image of one's future mate.)

We have reached the chimney & have stopped to contemplate its large mirror, surrounded by time worn gilding– On each side, a small silver candlestick, with a large one to take care of it– The middle of the chimney is always graced by a tumbler containing flowers, either fresh or faded, but more frequently the latter. . . . The chimney is not wanting in minor adornments, such as stray thimbles & wandering balls of cotton– Let us turn to the fire place– Do look at those massy andirons that seem to have been manufactured by the Cyclops– with tongs & shovel of an appropriate magnitude– then there is the little pair of bellows, which has served to inspire all the fires in the house for thirteen years. . . . And the new hearth brush, which our romping nieces are forbidden to ride, witch fashion, least they should discompose the symetry of its bristles– [S to H, 9 March 1830, quoting from "Our Parlour"]

On another occasion the Delaware governor's entourage provided Sophie with the subject for a hasty caric.

On Monday Papa announced to us that he was going to have our illustrious Governor, David Hazzard the 1st, (surnamed the <u>sheepface</u>) & several ostrogoths, to dinner!... it fell to <u>my lot to assist Frank</u> in this reception—Our Cousin was here by twelve, & we sat in <u>laughing</u> expectation of our <u>distinguished</u> guests till <u>one o'clock</u>, when "slow & with solemn pace" a <u>sulky</u> came in view.... Soon after a grand <u>scraping of feet</u> announced some important event—& Papa himself entered, escorting the Governor, next marched in Col. Potter, his aide de camp, & aide de camp general to all the governors since time immemorial, a huge old <u>original</u>, whose eccentricity nearly upset all our gravity—He called cousin nothing but <u>Col Du Pont</u> to Frank's great amusement. This is a little like him, only a <u>flattered</u> resemblance. [S to H, 13 September 1832]

The tracks of muddy feet and sparks from the ill-attended fires, along with Sir Sprol's cigar ashes, irritated poor Vic and threatened the carpets.

The carpets! These are many and varied—First is the green tissue from Lowell—Then, covering the middle of the apartment, the grey kersey from Louviers & near the fire, the little homemade rug of homeliest appearance—Not to count the inumerable rugs and strips, by doors and sofa and chimney.... But here comes Victorine, the eldest, and most important of all.... "Oh migh! look at this carpet full of mud–... The eldest seizes the shovel & begins sweeping the mud into it, with the brush—Meantime the fire–poor neglected fire—animated by the skillful pokes of the Lady Victorine, has begun to burn furiously—Suddenly a loud explosion is heard, & a shower of coal is cast over the carpets—Oh you girls, geese, little goats, can't you help me, cries Vic kicking with all her might—both the girls join, & by kicking stomping & scratching mutually impede each other—till the carpet being duly burnt & dirtied & the room perfumed with the odour of burning woolen, all is at last extinguished.

["Our Parlour", 2 March 1830]

FIXATIONS

*S*ophie endured the universal frustration of housekeeping—waiting for the repairman:

For I have been this whole morning in a state of mental & corporeal agitation, owing to the arrival of the painters & the non arrival of The Architect, to errect a scaffolding for their accomodation–The "deceitful monster" (I use lady Barcatus' vocabulary) Has been delaying this operation for the last two weeks, tho' "frequently & repeatedly" exhorted & admonished by every member of the family now at home–At length yesterday Papa insisted on his promising to appear at sunrise this morning, which he assured Papa he'd do–Conceive my state of vexation when I had the artists sur les bras, & still "he came not, sent not, faithless one!" I had to produce the chicken-coop bath tub &c &c on which ignoble object to commence their daubing–At length, at 12 oclock appears the architect, out of humour, with band of illnatured looking sattelites, & as there is great hostility between the knights of the brush & those of the saw, I am in constant expectation of new difficulties arising–It is in the midst of their tappage that I now write to you. . . . But you expect amusement from my letters, & I have chosen subjects far from suited to that theme–I will take a tour round the premises & look upon the ludicrous phyzes of the rival partisans, & perhaps catch inspiration to excite some gay or mirthful ideas in your mind–You will say I seek it in a very plebeian source– yet it is a lofty one, for the Carpenters sont à cheval sur des planches nearly as elevated as the summits of our piazza columns. . . . I am almost distracted by the weight of cares I have to support It will be necessary for me to rise at daybreak tomorrow. . . . My dear, I am quite disgusted with housekeeping 'tis a horrid employment! I shall not have that part of Tabby College to attend– [S to E, 12 June 1832]

Like most of her friends in the Society of Tabbies, Sophie steadfastly expressed her intent to remain unmarried. Yet even a spinster needed skills to manage a household.

Having served an observant apprenticeship in each of the major housekeeping departments, Sophie was well prepared to assume leadership during the Great Housecleaning of 1832, while her sisters were away.

My chief occupation has consisted since my return, in fixations, having arrived in the midst of that most unpleasant transaction, housecleaning, which however, you know is a necessary spring ceremony– [S to H, 21 April 1832]

Chimneys were swept. Then everything in the house was laid bare at one time. Blankets adorned the windows temporarily while curtains were laundered; aged pocket handkerchiefs ("pockos"), mittens, stray needles, and papers were removed from the back of the sofa; and smoky walls were whitewashed or painted. Sophie had been trained to the whole routine under the martial management of Victorine, and she longed for her sister to return home to resume supervision of the household:

> *Brought up as I have been in the Centre of a large family, the small circle to which it has been reduced of late years, does not prevent my feeling sensibly the absence of all other inmates save myself & uncle in our home—I hope to see Victorine return on Saturday, and am delighted with the idea of enjoying her society once more, as well as being released from the cares of housekeeping to which I am not at all partial—* [S to H, 30 May 1832]

As a child, Sophie had enjoyed the household activities in which she participated.

> *I have just been assisting sister to make some jumbles for you, which I know you will like. . . . David Murphy has put two small brass hoops on the largest of my three churns so that I can make butter in it without spilling the cream. . . . I wish you could be here to help us die the eggs and play with them.* [S to E, 18 April 1821]

Her skill in needlework had enabled her to coach Henry in sewing for the baby house, as she reminded him:

> *Do not you find your needles and thread very useful? I should think from the skill you displayed in those dear hours bygone, when you used to hem towels for our garret establishment under my tuition, that you would be very successful in mending any particularly obnoxious <u>hole</u>.* [S to H, 9 July 1829]

Her assessment of her skill in quilting was untinged by her customary modesty:

> *Today, Meta has a quilting frolick, and we are to read up there. So that I expect every minute to be interrupted by a summons to go there, for as I am a <u>great quilter</u>, Meta will not dispense with my assistance.* [S to H, 24 June 1828]

But after Sophie was swept into the world of books and drawing, her stitchery suffered. Victorine remonstrated from Philadelphia:

> *Pray Sophia what are you doing at your needle? I hope you use it a little more effectually than you did for some time before I left home?* [V to E and S, 1827?]

A Scene in peach season

The pleasure of eating clingstones—

[*V°*] 1 *Elenora* "*Oh I cant get far enough out of the window! What shall I do!*

2 *Vic*
3d *Soph* } *both mute, their mouths being full of peaches—*

I am obliged to be very careful of my diet, and not to eat any fruit, although the temptation is great here, there are so many peaches,
we have some now very nice and ripe, I venture to eat one at a time, but everyone here eats them by the half dozen—

[V *to* META, 11 September, 1829?]

Sophie never shared her sisters' enthusiasm for the latest fashions. She had to be prodded to send a report on the new styles in Philadelphia, even when she was busy filling Vic's and Tat's shopping orders and dashing in and out of stores. Happy as she was to keep her needle flying as she embroidered collars, trims, and handkerchiefs as gifts for her family and friends, she was reluctant to dedicate her efforts to dressmaking or designing. That she left to Vic and Tat.

Scene 4ᵗʰ

The morning's amusement (ie) Trying on dresses

1ˢᵗ   *Vic "Well! I think it sets well—dont you Mrs. W?"*

2ᵈ   *Mrs. W. "Oh I reckin it'll do now—see here is this the right length"*

                (measuring the hem)

3ᵈ   *Tat "I like my jigs exceedingly—they are much prettier than Sophs"*

I am now very busy cutting out work for Mrs Waterman, for I want her to alter some of our dresses before she goes to New York to pay her son a visit which will be about the 15ᵗʰ & as she will be away some weeks it is very important that she should fix at least part of our Summer clothes before her departure— [V to E, 6 May 1828]

Any way she could be useful to Papa gladdened Sophie's heart. Whether it was stitching cartridge bags, cutting out powder labels, sorting mail, or acting as copyist, she regarded it as a privilege:

Remember, my dear brother, that our parents have worn out the brightest years of their life toiling for us—they are now infirm and old—we cannot hope that they will be spared to us many years longer—and it is our duty to render their latest years as happy as we can, and to give them no cause of sorrow which it is in our power to prevent—

[S to H, 16 November 1827]

Mary Lowery, the daughter of that Lowery who used to live here & now lives at Youngs, is coming to live at our house—She comes on Monday. Jane is still our cook—Our other girl is Ann McGran. [S to H, 31 October 1829]

Cherry bounce   Scene II

1   *Eh, Moderation, Moderation. you stuff it too much*

2   *O pound   pound*

3   *Eleuthera–*

Second scene of Cherry bounce–Scene 3–

1st   *Eh! Je me sauve   je me sauve*

2d   *Ah que faire! vous m'abandonne*

1   *Lotte– I declare you shall go, you must–*

2^d   *Soph   No I wont, I cant, oh you wretch how can you try to hold me!–*

      Lotte   I'll make you go!

      Soph   no! that you wont, I'm off–

[V°]

Skirmish on the march to fortress Monroe

Half a dozen Irishmen pounding sausage below–

Dinner mounting–

1   *Lotte–Oh Bribe the cook not to send up the dinner*

2   *Soph (faintly)   Oh Hannah, cant you not bring up that pudding yet!*

      Lotte   Take it back! take it back!

      Soph–No, it will be cold, we cant go–

Transvasing the currant wine

[*V°*]   *Vic,   O! Jeremiah! If I only had a funnel!*

          Soph (gravely) "Vic If I bend this the least bit, I'll empty it all down your back—

          Vic   "You little wretch! I'm spilling! I'm spilling! hush! hush!

The bursting of the demiJohn—

[*V°*]   *The bursting of a demijohn into which Vic was pounding a cork—*

The bursting of the jug

[*V°*]   *1st Vic, 2d Soph, 3d Jane, all three squaling for help*

4th Mary Kelly, 5th Nancy, rushing to their assistance—

I have laughed so much today, that I am almost sick—You must know sister Vic has been transvasing her currant wine today and I was called in to assist in the operation. I supported the Demi John in my arms while Vic, squatted on the floor, filled the bottles. "O Jeremiah! cries she If I had but a funnel" "Sister, observed I, If I incline this the least bit, I could pour the whole down your neck." "You little wretch! hush! hush! I'm spilling!" I'll never have bottles enough" at the same time with a "switch of her tail," overthrowing one and breaking it to atoms! In this style she went on, till to my great relief all the bottles were filled. After dinner she went up into her room to cork them, but I declined being of the party. I was sitting in the parlour, when the most dreadful screams of "Help! help! Mary! help! assailed my ear I rushed to the pantry whence the sounds proceeded and beheld Vic the picture of despair, supporting in her arms a burst jug, from which torrents [of] wine were descending—Jane, who had reached the scene of action before me, was holding a plate under it, and both she and Vic screaming a qui mieux mieux. I, wishing to render all the assistance in my power, instantly joined in the chorus, (particularly as I beheld the plate overflowing) Our united efforts soon brought the rest of the household—"A bucket! a bucket! fetch a bucket," shrieked Mary Kelly—"A pitcher" cried Nancy "Anything," said Vic "Another plate" responded I—Mary Kelly precipitated herself with a pitcher full of water to receive the descending flood "You goose! no water! no water! you'll ruin it" cried Vic—What shall I do! says Mary. by this time the confusion became so great, everyone rushing against each other and screaming out at once that I fled—leaving them to do the best they could and they succeeded in securing part of the wine. The worst of the affair is that it is Mrs Lammots jug to which this bursting adventure happened. . . . [S to E, November 1827]

Sophie was intrigued by the commercial language of Papa's business correspondence. She reported that she had been

> *appointed Post Mistress of the Establishment. I have made a box with two compartments one entitled "Louviers"*
> *the other "Kirk & Co." in these the letters are put as soon as they come, and I send them when called for—I have also*
> *made a kind of rack to put the letters in that are to go to the post—the latter stands on the chimney in Papa's room*
> *My salary is the privilige of reading all the Newspapers!* [S to H, 5 November 1829]

Of the myriad tasks to be accomplished by the novice housekeeper, Sophie preferred taking care of the books, newspapers, and pamphlets. During one summer she undertook to fit protective covers on all the novels in the house. She labored hard moving all the many bound volumes in the family library when it was discovered that they were getting damaged on the ground floor:

> *We have been employed for two or three days in arranging the libraries and transporting the bound books upstairs,*
> *because they were getting spoiled down stairs.* [S to H, 15 April 1827]

She organized all the pamphlets in the closet so that they were retrievable, then waged her personal war on the aggressive mice and rats that dared gnaw at their edges. To ensure victory, she used every type of mouse and rat trap she heard recommended or could find. She even built her own:

> *On Saturday afternoon, Mary came to our house—I was making mousetraps (elegant employment for a lady) &*
> *had my wood & choppings all about—* [S to H, 27 January 1831]

To annihilate the annoying creatures she readily called on the household cats, as well as every tool imaginable, from pocket handkerchiefs to tongs. To Sophie the tongs were among the most useful implements in the house. Her first poetic efforts in 1823 included an "Ode to Tongs," and more than once she depicted their being used, in parlor and kitchen alike.

The kitchen was in no way Sophie's domain. She was perfectly content to leave the preparation of food to the cook and her team of two helpers. Lecturing Henry on maintaining a proper attitude toward servants, she revealed her own prejudices and her standards:

Accustomed to think their superiors in fortune must be their superiors in knowledge, propriety & manners, they necessarily will conclude that whatever they see them do, is right & proper, or at least excusable—therefore we should be careful to set a good example to our servants and inferiors—not for their sakes only, but for our own—since we depend on them for a great many of our comforts, and besides none are so prone to notice our failings as they are—We should be kind and considerate for them, & "give unto them that which is lawful & right, knowing that 'we' also have a master in Heaven—" [S to H, November 1829]

Sophie acknowledged that the special cooking was better left to Tat, whose talents in the culinary department were undisputed (especially appreciated were her gingerbread, pies, and preserves). Even the use of Papa's pumpkins she was happy to delegate to Tat and Lil.

Papa has a fine crop of yankee pumpkins with which Eleuthera has made some very tolerable pies. . . . Lil has succeeded in making his pumpkin seeds taste just like ground nuts— [S to H, 31 October 1829]

In the kitchen, as in the stitchery arena, Sophie preferred to stand by and help when needed. By the same token, the gardening was for Vic and Uncle to debate and attend to. The various du Pont households on the Brandywine proudly produced Cherry Bounce to enliven their tea fights, and sister Vic's currant wine was legendary.

As always, Sophie followed her own dictum in dealing with fixations:

Whatever is our duty, you know we must bear it with cheerfulness and strive to do our best— [S to H, 12 June 1829]

Yet, describing her situation to Henry, she complained:

Sister Victorine has been obliged to return to Philadelphia, & to leave me to enjoy the same state of solitude in which I have been for the last three weeks. Every situation my dear Harry has its cares & trials—& I do not know whether the duties of providing for the family & attending to the household matters as well as all connected with it, are not as difficult & fatiguing to me, as your drills & military duties are to you—It is also a responsible situation, since the comfort of others, & the wellbeing of the whole establishment weigh on my inexperienced shoulders, & I must give an account to Vic of all intrusted to me— [S to H, 6 June 1832]

PETS AND PESTS

*F*rom Azore to Zelia in the deer park, from hummingbirds to flying squirrels in the house, pet mania gripped the Brandywine. A menagerie of dogs and cats, small woodsy creatures, injured or tamed, and the inevitable rats and mice and insects overran Eleutherian Mills. Lil's caged squirrels hung in the kitchen for warmth, his silkworms spun silk in the garret, his frog catching filled the pond presided over by Papa's Newfoundland geese. Mama's calves cavorted in the deer park; the deer invaded the sheep pen or climbed onto the piazza. Lady Lex, a cat more privileged than most, was banished from the dining room for attacking Tom the mockingbird while he feasted on cockroaches.

Sophie included a status report on the pets and pests in letters she wrote to brothers and sisters away at school. To Eleuthera she reported on her cat and kittens:

> *Mother Lex is well and she thinks we are obliged to nurse her on account of your absense; she is always in Vic's room and as soon as I or Victorine set down she is on our lap. The kittens, doves, &c are well.*
>
> [S to E, 12 January 1821]

By the time Henry left for Mt. Airy, the care and feeding of pets was routine:

> *Every day as soon as I have done breakfast I do the Doves. They are very well—Then I go and feed the Pupies, chickens, cats, &c. My chicken house is coming on very well. After dinner I carry a large milkpan half full of soup, meat, and all that is left from dinner, to the dogs. After they have done I play with them a little while, then I go and prevent the chickens from stealing Wasp's food while she is eating.* [S to H, November 1822]

For Henry, Sophie's letters invariably carried news of his horse, Sidney, and the other animals:

> *All the family of pets, biped and quadruped, feathered and furred, are in a perfect state of salubrity—Old Cupid continues the torment of our lives, Griffon fights the doves, the parrot squalls, Tom has lost his tail, in short they all remain as bad as ever.* [S to H, 25 December 1830]

In a family of seven children a diversity of pets was to be expected:

[*V°*]   *Alfred and Elenora rushing through the woods after the black cats.*

1st   Alfred—"Oh Nox, Nox! he'll be lost! Oh! Oh!

2d   Elenora—"Oh! Catalina! she'll be down at the other house! Oh, Alfred!

catch her! Oh Catalina! puss! puss! puss!

Messrs. Editors

I have often observed with surprise the propensity which many people have to foster and cherish animals of various sorts. In many instances this feeling springs from an amiable cause, that of a benevolence which seeks to extend itself to surrounding objects and to promote general happiness; but I think this taste may be indulged to too great an extent; for instance I am acquainted with a worthy family in our neighbourhood where this pet mania prevails in a high degree—Five or six cats are always to be seen running in various directions.

["The Tancopanican Chronicle," 11 October 1823]

Each member of the family has his own particular favorite. The eldest daughter delights in birds and generally keeps a large assortment hung about the rooms in cages; the son's affections were all centered in his horse, till lately when he has adopted a mischievous puppy which annoys the whole house. To the above named animals may be added a couple of tame deer, a large sheep dog and a whole army of white & black fowl, which are prized on account of their elegant top knots.—I must not omit the catterpillars which are carefully preserved in cages by the young Entomologist in the hope of rearing butterflies; nor the quantity of unhappy turtles which are doomed to languish penned up during several months each Summer, for the amusement of a boy of seven years old.

["The Tancopanican Chronicle," 24 October 1823]

Pet preferences were not necessarily shared among the numerous animal-loving inhabs. Sophie intensely disliked Vic's parrot.

I wonder I had not spoken to you of Vic's detestable little parrot—Papa got it in New York as we came home from New Haven—It was our travelling companion home, and attracted the admiration of all our steamboat companions. She does not talk, but only shrieks in the most horrible style. She and Tom are sworn foes. The other day she was out of her cage, (as she often is, being very tame, & her wings cut). She went to climb up Tom's cage, which, he justly considered an unpardonable insult, and sprang forward and caught her by the toe—Pol squaled for help, but Tom held on, till Vic, who doats on Pol, flew to her rescue, while Tat & I laughed till we could scarcely stand. The said Pol, as soon as she sees us coming to meals, begins fighting the door of her cage, & making a famous uproar, till Vic takes her out, and setting her on a chair by the table, feeds her. [s to h, 23 October 1829]

Though she dutifully cared for Pol when left in charge as housekeeper, Sophie resolved to break the habit of calling her friend Mary Simmons "Pol"

as it confounds her with the odious Parrot; and Uncle Charles calls her "the parrot's cousin."

[s to h, 28 November 1829]

Her intolerance of feathered pets included doves and peacocks.

Alfred has an addition to the annoyances of his house in the shape of a pair of peacocks. I think they are the most odious birds. . . . They have chosen their roost under Nora's window and wake her at peep of dawn with their Tartarean notes. [s to h, 6 June 1832]

When Ella and Uncle Charles attempted to save the ancient dove, Count, Sophie offered no assistance. But she labored lovingly to revive Lil's white rat:

Day before yesterday, when lil and I went to feed white rat, we found him dead in the bottom of the cage!! As you may suppose we were very sorry. We brought him in the house and just as we were going to take him to be stuffed, I thought I saw him breathe! We instantly forced his mouth open, and poured down some warm milk, we laid him by the fire on some cotton and silk, and after some time he opened his eyes. We kept warming and nursing him all morning, till at last he was alive enough to stand! . . . we laid him in a box near the fire—I went to give him some more milk, but he was so well restored, that he jumped out of the box with a horrid scream and ran all about the room— [s to h, 18 November 1825]

Ah, it will surely die!

[*V°*] *Ella with the old Count in her lap, exclaiming "Oh Soph! indeed*
it will die! It will surely die!–

Miss and Pallas both have pups, but I dont know how many Lil has kept. The rest of the pets are in their usual state
except Old Count (the dove) who expired on Sunday in Ella's [lap] She beheld him in the last agonies, snatched him
out of the cage carried him to the fire, & called for emetic and laudanum – I stood and laughed, while Sprol adminis-
tered to it some wine and sugar – but in vain – It died, to my great satisfaction, and the great consternation of the
household. [S to H, 5 February 1828]

[*V°*] 1st *Jane pounding the mouse with a log of wood.*

2^d *Mary Kelly screaming "Oh she's massacreing it. She's massacreing*
it! Miss Eleuthera! the tongs! the tongs!"

3^d *Eleuthera rushing with the tongs.*

4th *Rachel lighting them.*

5 *Soph witnessing the scene from the stairs—*

I must tell you I am becoming almost as expert a mouse catcher as yourself. I was setting in Vics room on Wednes-
day, when I he[ard a] noise in the closet, looking in I beheld six mice on the shelf, feasting. . . . Snatching up a pocket
handkerchief and a small bandbox (true ladies' weapons) I commenced a combat, and came off victorious, having
exterminated three of my enemies, and put the rest to flight. I have since put three more to death.

[S to H, 12 June 1829]

*Azore and Zelia are very amusing—they inhabit their new house
now and seem to think themselves of great consequence—*

[S to H, 27 January 1824]

The unanimous favorites among the pets were the deer. The antics of Azore and Zelia, with their fawns Hector and Zamor, were the subject of some of Sophie's most amusing carics. The spacious house that Papa had built for them was large enough to be shared with other pets:

I went the other day to see the puppies, with Alfred & the little girls—They are growing finely—Alfred handed them to me thro' the deer house window, which made me think of the days you used to hand me dear little Ross in the same manner—The children were greatly amused at the pups, Emma calls them "little pumpkins."

[S to H, 19 December 1829]

But two-legged intruders were quickly dispatched by Azore:

This morning the little Italian (you know, that <u>dwarf</u> who works in the refinery) went into the park to arrange something about the large well—Azore rushed on him, cut him severely on his breast and his leg—He came here to have his wounds dressed by Mama and notwithstanding the sympathy we felt for what he suffered, we could hardly help laughing at his description of the adventure—"He threw me down and gave me a somerset" &c &c "I went to *help myself over the fence, and the fellow came to help me" &c &c &c. The Park shellbarks are fully ripe, but Azore eats almost all that fall, besides which we are too much afraid of his lordship to trust ourselves long in his presence.* [S to H, 25 September 1826]

Even the piazza next to the deer park was not safe from Azore's forays.

The steps before the piazza are finished all to the banisters–Azore is continually mounting them–The other day the bench which stops up the way being a little pushed aside, Azore got on the piazza–He threw down one of Vic's flower pots and broke it all to pieces, after which ensued a great conflict between him and Uncle, Stephens, Lily, Vic, Tat, Mama and Dwarf–After having for some time gallantly defended himself against such a host of adversaries he was forced to retreat– [S to H, 18 September 1826]

The battle was renewed when another deer joined the group in the hillside park:

Our new deer, Fanny, is very annoying–She is constantly on the piazza, and seizes every opportunity of rushing into the house, and what is worse, is so tame that there is no frightening her away–Azor encouraged by her example, is almost always on the piazza, and if any thing is left on the entry windows, they seize & devour it–if not, they knock it down. [S to H, 9 August 1829]

Besides the deer in their elegant quarters, the most pampered pet was Eleu's greyhound, Bevis, a namesake of Bevis in Sir Walter Scott's *Woodstock* and the first, but by no means the last, of the species on the Brandywine. The breed became so popular with the du Ponts that a visitor to the company office reported that it was carpeted with greyhounds. In his mistress's absence, one Sunday morning Bevis attended the Sunday School, despite Sophie's efforts to send him home.

There is nothing in which I miss Vic more than in Sunday School, nevertheless we made out yesterday very well. . . . Oh, I must tell you of our dear Bevis' amiable conduct–As we were going to school, Pol and I, I perceived him following us! I attacked him with my parasol, declaring he should not come; just then he made a spring to one side, & flew barking on two persons who were just coming up the overcreek path–We instantly recognized Messrs. Boyd & McIlvaine–I appeased Bev, & told Boyd the reason of my combat with him which he had witnessed, whereupon he declared that Bev. always behaved well in school! & went on praising him, & concluding with exhortation,

"Now mind be a good boy today, Bevis." This so puffed up the conceited animal that I never saw him behave worse—He raised two <u>grand yellings</u> in the school, which stunned all our ears, besides various squalls & misdemeanors, which obliged poor Nora to put him out <u>five times.</u> [S to E, 28 May 1832]

Sophie often sought Henry's opinion on names for new members of the canine contingent:

I cannot keep the puppy like Pallas, because we want to keep a <u>dog</u>—The other one however is almost as pretty, & if I like it when it is larger I think we'll keep it—In that case, do you think "Herbert" would be a pretty name for it? or cannot you suggest some other one. They are neither of them so pretty as Roswell <u>Young</u> (for its the fashion here to call dogs by their masters names, for instance, Brandy <u>Williams</u>, Prince <u>Dixon</u>, Cupid <u>Bidermann</u> &c.)

[S to H, November 1829]

Tigrane

Scene 6ᵗʰ Rousseau enters the dining room in a fit—

1 Ah my gracious. Oh ho, ho-ho. The cats in a fit

2 Ah the poor kittens got a fit

3 Eh la pauvre petite bete!

I have great trouble every day with Doctor and the cats. He will feed them at every meal, thus not only spoiling the excellent education I have bestowed on them, but also greasing the clean floor in a most shocking manner. If I can get to table before him, I never fail to throw the four cats through the window, to the no small amusement of all the family, as the said intollerable quadrupeds invariably reenter by way of the kitchen. [S to H, 20 February 1826]

Finding names for the numerous feline population, who roamed freely in and out the house, was up to Sophie. To reduce their number, she regularly had them transported across the creek:

> *I sent Erminia over the creek some time ago but this morning she arrived home! We don't know how she did it unless she got in the boat.* [S to H, 22 October 1823]

It was Papa who saved one cat from exile among the overcreekers:

> *We have a little cat I call Griffon, but instead of assisting me, he spends all his time at the Dovecage, tormenting Zize pampan—He would long since have been exported to Louviers, (that Botany Bay of our cats) had not Papa taken him under his especial protection of late.* [S to H, 19 December 1829]

As ratcatchers, the cats were a cowardly lot—"pusillanimous wretches," Sophie called them. They seemed quite content to inhabit a peaceable kingdom "overrun with Rats, mice, cats & kittens, who all live in peace & amity together." Sophie longed for Henry, "prince of ratcatchers," to attack the rodents.

> *The Rats, aware I suppose, of your absence, have taken up their winter quarters in our house in such numbers that they almost distract Mrs. Waterman. They gnaw her clothes, and come walking over the bed at night, and make the greatest possible tappage all over.* [S to H, 31 October 1829]

At last, in spite of a vast assortment of mousetraps and the valiant efforts of Sir Sprol, who sent many a foe to the shades, tragedy struck the besieged household. The rats attacked Vic's parrot.

> *Polly is no more! The gentle, melodious peruche was assassinated last Friday night! Do not suspect me of the deed, I assure you I was not at all accessory to it—at midnight, when all were wrapt in peaceful slumber, Sir Sprol having an attack of insomnia, was startled by faint shrieks in the parroquet language, issuing from the dining room—The heroic youth started from his couch, & without donning his armour, snatched up a falchion (ie the poker) & taking a light in the other hand, rushed to the rescue—he found the innocent victim vainly struggling with a huge rat! His interference caused the monster to desist & fly, but his speed was no security against the valour of his antagonist, who, with a successful thrust of his noble weapon, stretched him lifeless on the plain—The unfortunate Peruche survived her wounds only half a day!—I wrote the news to Vic, & was so grieved to think of her despair, that I actually could not touch my breakfast after I heard of the catastrophe!* [S to E, 28 May 1832]

A hunting piece.–

On the night of the 15th Inst. after the family of Anthy J. Bidermann
had retired to rest, Mrs. B–was alarmed by strange noises in her chamber She arose and struck a light, when to her utmost terror and surprise
she beheld–a Butterfly of the largest size! . . . This should serve as a
caution to housekeepers to guard carefully their doors & windows lest
such dangerous animals should enter–

["The Tancopanican Chronicle," 20 September 1823]

*Enter lady Eleuthera singing in triumph
the Marseillaise hymn
"Le jour de gloire est arrive"–
War of the Wasps*

[*V°*]

War of the Wasps
Soph–Oh most valiant Rodrigo, you'll be strong!
Tat–No, no, hold here the vase, quick Ive secured the foe–

I must tell you a scene that occurred last night—I was retiring to my apartment (the <u>passage room</u>) by way of <u>Vics</u>, when I beheld a huge rat walking up the three steps into my room, very deliberately. As I knew there were no holes in my room, I stepped up & closed the door behind him, ran down, seized <u>Abra</u>, & alarming Vic & Tat, we all three hastened to my room, where we soon discovered the foe, on the steps between the two rooms, we instantly shut the other door, first throwing <u>Abra in</u>, & left <u>ces deux fiers animaux</u> as Le Vaillant would say, shut up together—In vain we expected to hear the combat, Abra would not touch nor approach the rat—Down to the cellar we flew for Griffon, who kicked and scratched most furiously when in our paws, but no sooner was the pusilanimous wretch placed in vue of the foe, than she shrunk in the corner by Abra's side & would not touch him, tho' the rat enraged & terrified, ran screaming <u>over</u> & <u>over</u> the two cats! Vic attempted to <u>fight him</u> with the <u>tongs</u>, I with a stick of wood, but being both (shall I confess it?) rather daunted, Tat was ordered to dismount the window where she had taken refuge, & go for Papa—He made his appearance with the broom stick, & a tremendous engagement ensued, between the infuriated animal & Pa & Vic, with tongs & broom, while Tat & I, on beds & windows, holding candles, at once illuminated & encouraged the combatants. At last Pa laid the monster low, with a successful thrust of the broomstick!

[S to H, 21 April 1832]

A lesson in Fencing.

[V°]   1   Vic–Oh Elenora, do teach Joan to jump fences! did you ever see
                   any one get over in such a style?

       2ᵈ Joan–"Oh I'm stuck fast, I cant go back or forwards–

       3ᵈ Nora–"Here, hold out your foot, take courage & do it gracefully,
                 like Mrs. Bauduy!

[V°]

1 Elenora–Who Wha! yow! ho!
         Oh! ha ha ha!

2 Eleuthera "Oh James fly to the rescue!"

3ᵈ James "Wait I'm coming to you!–

COUNTRY DIVERSIONS

Sophie understood the countryside around her. She knew the flora and fauna well; she relished the change of the seasons; she sought to share the delights of a rural existence with her city friends who came to visit. Granted, she demonstrated considerable intolerance toward urban acquaintances like the giggling Misses Cruger, who were frightened by grazing cows. And she laughed at friends who had to be taught the art of graceful fence climbing. But the readiness of young Smiths, Lammots, and Cazenoves to participate whole-heartedly in the country diversions of the Brandywine won for them Sophie's loyal and lasting affection.

During the cold months the excitement of sleighing, snow forts and battles, ice-skating, and filling the icehouse relieved the tedium of indoor life.

One Sunday Alfred took us on the ice. Poly first went on the chair and Alfred pushed her. Brother B. arrived just as they returned and he pushed me. Poly went to slide. I turned my head to look at her, when lo she fell down on her nose!! she was not in the least hurt and we laughed very much. Afterwards Pol went again on the chair and then we came home. I was fortunate enough not to fall, though it is true I did not try to slide. [S to H, 13 February 1823]

Sophie was less interested in the distance skating that captivated both Alfred and Brother.

Last Sunday, Alfred and Brother Bidermann rode to Wilmington, taking with them their skates, and skated up the Christina till far above Newport—12 miles—They intended to have gone as far as Christiana bridge, but as they wished to be home in time for dinner, they thought it would take them too long. They say thay had delightful skating. . . . Lil bids me tell you that yesterday Alfred, "skating on the creek," cut <u>129</u> outside strokes without stopping. [S to H, 2 5 January 1 8 2 7]

Nor was she nearly so adventurous as Lil, who—once given skates—tried them on the allées of the garden and on the storm-created pool beneath the pantry window, as well as on the creek.

The number of Eleutherian Mills visitors diminished in winter, when the steamboat from Philadelphia was often locked in by ice, but friends enlarged special wintry excursions nonetheless.

Tat, Meta, Alfred and M^r R Smith made a party to go up the creek far above Youngs, to see a dam of ice which is said to be a great curiosity—Ella accompanied them and they had a great deal of fun—The ice dam, they say, consists of monstrous pieces of ice, larger than our dining table, which are piled one above another for a great distance. They walked up on the ice nearly the whole way. [S to H, 2 5 January 1 8 2 7]

Even tea parties and special celebrations continued through the winter season. Just returned from Alexandria, Eleu

accompanied us to Meta's & we had a very pleasant party, for the happiness of seeing her again made us all very merry. There was no one there besides the Gilpins & us except Caroline Morris & Ella. <u>Uncle Charles</u> was our sole <u>beau</u>. Was it not wonderful he condescended to come to a teaparty? That day the Miss Gilpins spent here, & slept here that night, as their roads are impassable after night. In the morning we had just been talking of how very long it was since we had seen Wilhelmina Young when looking through the window, we beheld her in propria persona! She gave us a description of their amusements on Evans' birthday & told me they <u>danced in the grist mill</u> till 5^1/$_2$ in the morning! [S to H, 1 2 January 1 8 3 1]

At the first snowfall, thoughts turned to sleighing:

Yesterday the first sight that met our eyes was the descending of a considerable fall of snow. We were glad for we were wishing for sleighing. In the afternoon the snow ceasing, Joliecoeur put the greys in the sleigh, & Eleu & I embarked with Charlotte & Tom Smith, neither of whom had been in a vehicle of the kind before. We went to Wilmington, rode down one St & up another & came straight home. The sleighing was not very good on the turnpike, but we had a pleasant ride. [S to H, 27 December 1831]

Papa had purchased a new sleigh for the family just after the Brandywine endured the worst blizzard since 1760. Describing the event, Sophie wrote:

Torrents of snow made their way into the house through our delightful Boydish *windows, till in several rooms it reached & covered a part of the floors.* [S to H, 20 January 1831]

I think you would laugh very much to see James Bidermann driving Annette to a sleigh! (a candle box) We saw her yesterday creeping along at the rate of a mile in four hours – yet James declares she ran off with him five times *&* upset him four! *He is in the pride & joy of his heart, driving a sleigh with his* fleet courser. [S to H, 29 December 1831]

The snow fell from Friday to Monday afternoon, leaving drifts some ten feet deep, and no road was cut through to Wilmington until Tuesday afternoon. The new sleigh, for one or two horses and five passengers, was heavily used that winter, prompting Sophie to write wistfully to Henry:

> *I often wish you were at home to enjoy the Sleighing—had you been here, I suppose I should have had some famous upsets, as all the others would have been afraid to trust to your driving, I suppose, & I should not. . . . Last Saturday & sunday the wind rose & drifted our lane & the new road full of snow again—Alfred & Brother who didnt know this persuaded Tat & Mary Lammot to go out a little way sunday afternoon, & they had the pleasure of seven upsets! . . . Bevis always follows us when we go sleighing, the snow & the sound of the bells delight him—*

[27 January 1831]

Even when the weather was abominable, Sophie tried to walk outside, sometimes conducting a piazza parade. Yet a severe winter hampered a regimen of daily exercise, so as eagerly as she had anticipated the snows she longed for the end of winter and the sight of the first spring blossoms.

Sleighing, "mieux tard que jamais"–
Snow invisible, mud abundant–gridirons & porringers abroad–

On Friday we had a furious snow storm all day, the snow fell very deep & we thought on Saturday, as it cleared beauteously, that we should have splendid sleighing–But alas! 'twas as mild as summer–Still the depth of snow was such, that we deemed it could not soon melt, & at eleven o'clock Nora & I embarked with Pa & Joliecoeur for our little city. . . . We had a horrid time shopping, I never scudded thro' such streets! the gutters torrents, the eaves cascades, the pavements slush, the crossings mud, & snowballs flying like hail thro' the atmosphere, impelled by the rude hands of troops of imps, & men, shouting & bawling & making as much noise as possible–by the time we could come home, the snow had dissolved into slushy mud, & such a ride as we had! . . . every thing on runners was abroad, from splendid yellow & red equippages, to gridirons, porringers & frying pans.

[S to H, 19 February 1833]

The time for long, uninterrupted days of reading or sewing by the fireside is past now—& I expect my books & my needle will have a frequent holiday—in truth, we <u>country-folks</u> are very like the <u>snakes</u> of our woods, which immerge from their holes to enjoy the first warm sunbeams— [S to Clementina Smith, 13 March 1832]

Explorations in the surrounding woods and creeks were limited in good weather only by the condition of Sophie's knee and the availability of a companion. She found it far more entertaining to share her promenades, and the young people of her Philadelphia coterie enthusiastically joined her. Sometimes a refreshing, jewel-like spring prompted a reflective pause in the day's rambles, or a fallen limb beside a fence suggested an impromptu seesaw. Sensitive to the beauty of the bouldered valley, they gave free rein to the romanticism of their age:

At five o'clock we sallied forth, and repaired to the spring in the clearing, which is now lovelier than I ever saw it— The Dogwood and hawthorn are in bloom all around it, and their white blossoms contrast beautifully with the varied green of the young leaves, that just begin to throw a shadow over the thousand flowers that bloom beneath them. The loud singing of the birds, added to the trickling of the fountain through the moss, and its dashing over the rocks on the hill below, formed a music far more melodious to my ear, than that of fifty Oratorios could possibly be— Ella and I sat there till sunset and I dont know when we have had more fun—We had fifty little adventures, such as my dropping my gloves into the fountain, and not perceiving it till they were soaked through &c

[S to E, 8 May 1828]

One day last week Nora and I went over the creek & walked to the <u>dolphin</u>, you have been there no doubt, & know what a beautiful, romantic spot it is—I climbed rock after rock, & stood surveying the wild scenery around, so congenial to my taste & feelings, & delighted by the dash of the water round & below me, till Nora remarked we might catch the <u>ague</u> in that damp place, which unsentimental recollection induced us to leave it—On our road home we came to a fence over which an old log was laying—this we drew to the middle, & each mounting an end enjoyed a good <u>seesaw</u> for about half an hour, much in the style represented in this beautiful sketch—Both singing in chorus with such delightful melody, that the very <u>ground squirrels</u> came out to listen! Do not suppose however that we were in danger of having any other <u>auditors</u> or spectators, for we were in a very wild spot, or you may be sure would not have done thus— [S to H, 5 October 1831]

Some wooded walks were a necessary part of calling on neighbors or Sunday School pupils on either bank of the Brandywine, for visiting was a major diversion of the countryside.

On Thursday Tat Lil and I determined to go and spend the day at Pol's. . . . Papa insisted on our all three going in his gig, Riley leading the horse—we presented a truly comic appearance, Tat and I on the seat; I, loaded with portfolios, crayon cases &c for drawing; Tat, with a bundle of stockings to darn and a story she took for us to read— Between us, aloft in awful state on a barrel of pears and melons, sat Alexis, armed with the net to catch insects, which floated like a pennen in triumph over the horse's head. Everyone we met was in a roar and I was nearly convulsed with laughter—To add to the fun I discovered Tat had brought the 2nd volume for the first, so we could not read! We had nevertheless a most  *delightful day.* [DIARY, 30 August 1827]

Spontaneous, casual gatherings were far more agreeable to Sophie than the stiffer, more formal tea parties that increased in frequency as the young people matured.

Oh dear! The very thought of it puts me in a persperation! To have to exert yourself to laugh & talk & look so gay & merry, when you feel exactly the reverse, & this hot weather too! But 'tis the way of the world.

[S to H, 15 August 1831]

She learned to endure the tea fights of necessity; they were after all a sociable way to recognize the presence of houseguests in the neighborhood.

We have hardly known what to do with ourselves, but today is worst of all, & I only hope you have it cooler at the Point. We had a <u>stewing</u> time at our tea fight on Monday, but all went off very well indeed, every one appeared to enjoy themselves; notwithstanding the heat, we danced to the Piano after part of the Company had gone—The girls all waltzed, I wish you could have seen Elenora & Clementina waltzing together, they are as light & graceful as two fairies—But after it was over they looked like drowned Rats and scampered off to bed in short order.

[S to H, 19 August 1831]

Far more enjoyable were the outdoor activities of summertime. When Sophie was about ten years old, Papa had built his daughters a bathhouse on the creek bank. After it was destroyed by the freshet of 1822, it had to be rebuilt.

> *Papa has had a delightful bath house built for us in the powder yard—But we have not been able to enjoy it much this summer. It is a very large one, and very convenient being so near the house; we have only to walk down the hill to get to it.* [S to H, 19 August 1828]

The structure with its dressing area was strictly for the women of the family. The men swam separately, skinny-dipping in the creek or in a millrace. This could lead to a crisis, as Alexis discovered when he was interrupted by a thunderstorm.

[*V°*]   *1st*   *Ella flying after old Mother Powers*

         2d   *M*rs *Powers hobling along pulling up her stockings and*

                exclaiming "I declare, I didnt get time to put on my garters!—

                                      May 11th 1828—

[*V°*]　*Valiant conduct of the Lavatory Company, on the Invasion of the Ganders.–*

1　*Skearquick "Get out." How dare you come here!"*

2　*"Laughing shriek (from behind the curtain) "Go away this minute, you impertinent fellows."*

3ᵈ　(Elisa) "Ah Ha! girls, its only the geese!"

When Joanna returned from her ride, she & I went down to the bath house where we met Elisa. . . . During our bath what should Joan do in some of her evolutions but pull down one of the boards at the side of the bath house fronting the opposite bank of the race! of course it exposed us to the view of any who might come there – we however thought no one would – suddenly I beheld someone, I screamed to the girls & we began scrambling up the stairs all at once pell mell – I was the last & had hardly gained the ascent, before a tremendous plunge was heard, & the next minute an immense mass was in the bath house – "Get out of here this minute" cried I indignantly, thinking it was a troop of boys, but when our terror a little subsided, we beheld the whole flock of Geese, which some one from the shore, with stones & sticks, compelled to swim to & fro in our bathing space! . . . On returning home we found it was Alexis & Harriet Cazenove who had driven them in as a trick & an excellent one it was, for it "skeared" us finely.

[S to H, 26 August 1831]

Lil went bathing with Alfred near the dam. When it began raining Lil jumped out, put on his hat and shoes, and taking his clothes on his arm ran stark naked to the refinery. Unfortunately he happened to rouse Alfred's 34 geese, who set off full gallop after him. It must have been very funny to see Lily running naked through the powder yard with the geese all screaming at his heels. [S to H, 23 June 1825]

Refreshments

We were down at the <u>Lavatory</u>, where we had a great deal of fun as usual—
It is this year beset by <u>Spiders</u>, to our great horror—

[S to H, 15 July 1830]

Lil's tutor, Mr. Rice, also came to woe when he trekked to the millrace for his customary nighttime bath.

> *They have been repairing the race at Hagley this week, & it has been emptied & the mills stopped—I must tell you a good one of Rice—the first day of these reparations, he went to bathe as usual at 11 oclock at night, & not knowing the race was emptied, repaired to his usual bathing place, and sprang in—Conceive his dismay when he found himself floundering in thick mud! at the bottom! He scrambled out as well as he could & crawled into the creek, where he got rid of the coat of mail (ie mud) with which he was surrounded—He is a great oddity & very amusing—*
>
> [S to H, 3 September 1831]

Rowboats on the creek provided another respite from the summer heat—except for the oarsman.

> *Lil rowed us up nearly to the bridge one night last week—but we knew Miss Young was in Phil.ª so we did not stop— Lil rows very well, & so does Elenora considering she's a girl—I tried, but they would'nt teach me how to turn the oar, so I made but a poor hand at it—* [S to H, 28 September 1830]

Lil spent much of his free time on the river fishing, or frogging along its banks. His catch usually reappeared on the dinner table, but occasionally he was overly zealous in his expeditions:

> *Lil and James . . . went frogging the other day & caught 54!* [S to H, 15 August 1831]

Using a blowgun, he hunted birds and small animals as well. Sophie did not sympathize with his hunting activities; she feared the Brandywine would lose all its amphibians if Lil continued to shoot, and she vastly preferred his seeking to expand his collection of Indian darts.

The young women of the Brandywine had considerably less liberty than Lil in their daily diversions, a situation Sophie deplored.

> *I have been but once to Glentivor since the girls are here. I have been very anxious to go, but have always had something to prevent me—Ellinora has been sitting with me all afternoon, taking care of [her stepbrother] Robert, who is as cross as the very mischief, or as "ten Cats" as Elli is justly remarking—M.ʳˢ L[ammot] is gone to Lenas, and we both wish the urchin in Jericho with all our hearts, as we want to go and eat currants in the garden—*
>
> [S to H, 15 July 1827]

[*V°*]   *Descent to Veolan Bower   August 31ˢᵗ 1831*

1   *Joan screaming "Oh! I'm down again! I cant get up! help me, you creature!–"*

2ᵈ   *Soph–"My dear, that comes of drinking so much wine at dinner! here's my*
        hand–jump up–"

Joanna & I passed the morning reading Waverly & discussing peaches, as all the rest were gone out–after dinner she
& I went & took a lovely long walk–We went to the Lovers Cliff, & from thence some way along the brow of the hill,
& then tried to descend it–but ere we descended half way, Joan managed to prostrate *herself three times, so we*
concluded to retrace our steps after resting amid a group of dogwood trees, a sweet spot which we named Veolan
Bower, to comemorate our reading Waverly–Joanna was so fortunate as to take but two more sittings in reascending
the hill, but accomplished a fifth ere we stood on the summit of the "hill of flowers" near Crevice run–

[S to H, 3 September 1831]

[*V°*]   1. *Eleuthera*   *Oh Pruderino do help Miss Lammot*

          2. *Pruderino*   *"Do take my arm, miss"*

          3. *Elenora*   *"Oh no! you are too Low!"*

          4. *Pruderino*   *"Then lean on my shoulder, thats better—"*

          3. *Elenora—*   *"Yes thank you!"*

On Saturday afternoon Prudencio Santander came out to see us, & Vic asked him to stay till Monday, which he did.
He inquired much after you—He has heard that his guardian Dr. Colesberry will be home this fall, & also that his
family in Mendosa are well, so that he is very happy, & amused us by recounting his recollections of South America,
the Bull fights &c &c [s to h, 18 October 1830]

They were quick and imaginative in creating entertainment:

On Monday as it was raining the girls determined to have some fun indoors, & they & Alexis played all manner of tricks—they dressed up Harriet in Lils clothes, made pudding beds &c. . . . [S to H, 15 August 1831]

And on a summer evening they enjoyed their youthful freedom:

After supper the whole squad of us rushed into the garden, some to the swing, some to the pear trees, the moon was shining "hugely" as Mʳ Poe would say—Pol & I ran races, I came off victorious—at last at about ten oclock, Vic packed us all to bed— [S to H, 19 August 1831]

[*V°*]   *A new style for Swinging*

lady like pastimes

Uncle Charles has put up a delightful swing in the garden, between the two chesnut trees near the pump, and this, as you may suppose, affords us a great deal of amusement.
[S to H, 16 June 1828]

pleasures of returning from a tea fight

*pleasures of
returning from a teafight*

*pleasures of
returning from a teafight*

[*V°*]

Monday July 25th 1821
tea party at the Gilpins—return, twelve oclock—
doors locked—windows open—

Soph (in a tone of despair)—Oh I'll never scramble up,
its too high—
Nora (roaring) No no, take courage. see Im in,
its very easy—Pull up
your frock higher, Do like me—

A new plan to bear a lady over a fence—

Seeing the carpenters nailing has reminded me of Ellerslie. . . .
Our visit was—like our visits there always are—amusing without
being agreeable—When we set off on our return, "The knight &
lady fair" escorted us half way home! We came to a fence just near
the factory, on top of which two additional bars had been nailed to
prevent its being demolished—Ella ventured a hint on the renewed
difficulties the knight had had placed in our way, when he indig-
nantly sprang forward & with his fist broke down the bars, declar-
ing he did "not know who had done that"—His men looked
amused; perhaps he had himself given orders for it? Oh what
uncharitable suspicions! [S to E, 12 June 1832]

A new plan to bear a lady over a fence—

GUM ARABICS AND INEXPRESSIBLES

*N*avigating the rock-strewn country paths to call on neighbors or adventuring through the woods could prove hazardous. Once, berry-picking with Lil, Sophie had a near fatal encounter with a poisonous snake. Fortunately, crises were more often comical than serious.

Laughing while she and her companions struggled through muddy or snowy lanes, Sophie thoroughly exercised her "risibles" as well as her extremities. On these country walks proper young ladies suddenly found their petticoats and pantaloons—their "inexpressibles"—exposed for the world to see when they missed a stepping-stone in a stream or when their feet anchored in the mud.

The stylish pantaloons, often of lightweight cotton, provided protection as well as a decorative touch to the dress of the day. In cooler weather they were covered by an extra petticoat of flannel, besides the fancier petticoat that completed the array of inexpressibles. While visiting in Philadelphia, Sophie was shocked one morning to discover that she had neglected, in a moment of abstraction, to don her "flannels"—her extra flannel petticoat—and was about to go shopping without being fully dressed.

Dignity was more likely to be sacrificed in the country, where exposing inexpressibles was less distressing than tumbling down a hillside. Or not being able to climb it:

> *Have we not had the most enchanting Springlike weather for some days? It makes one wish to be <u>always</u> out of doors—The only draw-back is the walking, which affords no alternative between <u>snowy-ice</u> & deep, thick, mud—We manage to <u>wade</u> through it pretty well, with our Indian rubber shoes—Saturday Eleu & I were over the creek—The turnpike was one sheet of ice, at last in one place 'twas so slippery that we determined to mount in the woods—Just as Eleu was scrambling up thus,   on all fours, I laughing at her, up came Fountain, who grinned from ear to ear, & informed us, 'twas slippery! quel <u>nouvelle</u>!* [S to H, 9 March 1831]

Eleu fared less well the following winter when she and Sophie celebrated Washington's Birthday

> *by a parade to Mrs Siddals, thro' inexpressibly bad roads. It is the longest walk I've yet taken, & I am happy to say I bore it very well, tho' it was rendered doubly fatiguing by the mud, Eleu lost both shoe & india rubber, & soused*

her unprotected pedes in a <u>snow bank</u>! for there was a little of every thing on the surface of the earth then, snow

drifts, ice, water and earth in every stage of liquification– [S to H, 25 February 1832]

India-rubber overshoes, also known as gum arabics, were essential to excursions in bad weather. The first items collected in a rescue bundle for a group caught in a sudden shower were the gum arabics; then came the shawls.

They all three departed–and had not been gone an hour when it was pouring! Imagine sister Victorine's despair! At

last she dispatched Mullen loaded with Indian rubbers, shawls &c after these errant damsels, who availed them-

selves of an interval between the showers & arrived here towards evening without any inconvenience from the

excursion. [S to SFDP, 21 March 1833]

Scene 5th Going to a literary party

1   *I'm stuck fast in the mud*
2   *Come my dear do go on.–*
3   *Oh I've just extricated my foot*
4   *Ha. ha ha ha.–*

Brother and Evelina Victorine Mr Smith Alexis and I went together to the literary which was to be at Evelina's.
Meta and Alfred followed later. We read Lionel Lincoln and returned at 10 oclock. Alfred who carried the lantern
managed it badly as he did on the evening of Charles Cazenove and I should inevitably have made out as horridly as
we then did, had I not planted myself behind sister Victorine and Mr. Smith and profiting by their example avoided
all the puddles and stones over which they stumbled. [E to S, 13 March 1825]

Stepping oer a rivulet–

When we two wandered by the streams, or track'd them to their

source"   *Oct 13–1831*

[*V°*]   1   *Elenora Oh Soph   wait till I come to your assistance–*
2*d*   *Soph   "Oh wha! wha! wha! I'm* <u>sinking</u>

Lieut Hog & Dog–Hey, see what it is to have invention!
how finely I've got over it?–
Captain Spidersbane "Ah, by which end shall I touch it
not to dirty my fingers?"
General Skin & bones "Well–is the Captain going to
cross over on all fours, I wonder–"

[*V°*]

Pulling on rubbers under difficulties

In the afternoon Lina went over the creek by way of Youngs bridge, in the <u>Jumper</u>; *but they had passable sleighing as 'twas the bye roads— On Saturday Vic went for Pol in the dearborne, & she staid with us til Sunday afternoon. . . . She went to S. School, but* <u>rode</u>, *of course— we* <u>floated</u> *there, in Indian rubbers, thro' melted snow & mud—*

[S to H, 19 February 1833]

A winters walk to Billys—

1– "Courage. Now, Its not so bad–"
2 "March on, I'm after you–"

On Sunday there was a thunderstorm, quite severe for the season— And since then it has been quite cold & unpleasant—I never saw such walking as we've had—Sunday we rode to school in the cart, but walked home, or rather, slipped and sailed home, for I never saw such travelling. The whole road was composed of three delightful ingredients, sqush, slush, & mush—thro' which we boldly <u>dashed</u> *&* <u>splashed</u>, *sprinkling each other at every leap with liquid mud—You may think in what a state we got home.* [S to H, 9 March 1830]

A healthy supply of overshoes was kept on hand at Eleutherian Mills. But none could compare with the enormities worn by John Phillips; they were so huge Sir Sprol called them "les bottes de Polyphème." Of course Sophie caricatured them, along with their owner. But all the inhabs were intrigued by Phillips's experiments with the rubber material.

> *Have you heard of that new Invention for melting indian rubber, & extending it to any size, by steeping it in ether? Mr Phillips has been doing some, he showed us a large, <u>very</u> large bladder, quite transparent, & filled with air, which he had made out of a bottle of Indian rubber–Alfred had been trying to do some, & has been impesting us with the smell of ether, but I dont know how he succeeded–* [S to H, 17 April 1830]

In extremely cold weather gum arabics shielded the feet and hooded cloaks covered the head. But rain, snow, and chill winds sometimes necessitated even more protection. Sophie and her contemporaries knew how to adapt their hoods.

> *I wrapped myself up in an old black cloak & drawing the hood over my face, sallied forth. It was snowing <u>"like the mischief"</u> (elegant comparison!) so I pinned up my cloak hood in front, till nothing was visible but the tip end of my nose & two little eyes twinkling in the distance–* [S to H, 24 March 1831]

Such small beacons would have been a great help during some of the nighttime walks in the country. In the absence of moonlight, a lantern lit the way to literaries, where the du Pont men and women gathered to read aloud the latest novels. On one occasion, as Cousin Frank wrote to Sophie in May of 1833, he found his way home by the light of his own cigar.

> *I took off without a Lantern, & found myself soon engaged in impenetrable darkness on the turnpike. . . . My manner of getting along would have afforded the subject of a rich caricature–how do you suppose I managed–not quite on all fours, though very near to it–It was to a good & trusty cigar that I owed my safety–I would advance some ten paces, stoop down with my nose almost touching the ground, give three or four hasty puffs, which created sufficient light for me to recognize the stones & gullies–but for this I should have broken some of my limbs as sure as life–so commend me to a cigar all the days of my life–*

[V^o]

December 31st 1831 Saturday morning

A stroll to fortress Monroe–

1   *Soph* *"Ah migh Lotta, I wish we'd mounted*

               in the creeper!"

2   *Lotta* *"Oh my dear! its knee deep! do you*

               think the Doctor is peeping!"–

December 31st 1831 Saturday

December 31st 1831 Saturday

[V^o]

1   *Lotte–Ah look at our floor!*

           tis finely decorated!

2^d *Soph* *My dear, dont stop to admire,*

            quick quick put on yr stockings!

1   *Lotte–I'm drenched–*

2^d *Soph– So am I–Oh if Vic knew this!*

On the day before New Years, Alfred set out early in the morning with Alexis, in Tinshanks eggshell on runners, which he terms a sleigh, & proceeded to Lenni after Elenora. It snowed here furiously all day. . . . they came home just before dark–Alfred went to drive on to Metas, but Lo! just at the pigpen (sentimental spot!) down broke the equipage! & poor Nora had to scramble through snow knee deep, into the house! . . . Well, according to a good old custom, they insisted we must sit up to see New Years in–I objected at first for fear it would make us get up too late Sunday morning, however we concluded it would not have that effect & so sat up, discussing a dish of boiled Chesnuts, & a pitcher of very weak milk punch, a beveradge strongly recommended by our two physicians Drs Smith & Bauduy As it was 12 ere we parted in the parlour, it was two ere Lotte & I were consigned to the arms of Morpheus. . . . [S to H, 6 January 1831]

Since only a smooth roadway could minimize the hazards to walkers, the ladies of the Brandywine en masse petitioned for an improved path to their bathhouse on the riverbank:

To Alfred V. Du Pont Esqr–

Whereas the asperities, activities & declivities of the passage, road, or avenue, leading, conducting, & proceeding to the Tancopanican Lavatory, do greatly severely & continually incommode, disturb, & agitate, the frames, feet & breath of the Lavators, Visitors, & others, walking journeying or travelling the said passage, road, or avenue, we the undersigned, visitors of the Tancopanican Lavatory, do humbly petition, urge & request you, head of the engineer department of the Tancopanican, to order, despatch & send, a detachment of pioneers, surveyors, labourers & all needful weapons, to open, clear, & aplanate said passage, road, or avenue–& whereas we the undersigned lavators, visitors & others, do intend, purpose & design, daily, frequently, & repeatedly, to walk, journey & travel by said passage, road, or avenue, we urge, request, & entreat, that it be improved, amended & aplanated, with alacrity, speed & expedition–signed V E Bauduy–S. M. Du Pont

Eleuthera Du Pont   M. E. Simmons   G. J. du Pont   E. A. Lammot   M. E. du Pont.

Their eloquence produced results. The path to the bathhouse smoothed, the young ladies, attired in their gum arabics, inexpressibles, frocks, shawls, and bonnets, could safely march down for a summer swim. Sophie's caric of one such Progress prompted Mrs. R. Smith to confess to Tat that she had "seen the Lavatory Marching Company, and this is a strong whet to my desire to see more."

[*V°*]   *Band playing the Lavatory company's* <u>March</u>

Interlude, 1st   Capt Spiders bane—Oh! I'm stuck fast.

2d   Lieut Hog & Dog—"Oh my dear are my regimentals high enough" such mush

3d   Lieut Skearquick—"Truly Captain, the parade ground's rather <u>soft</u> my clean inexpressibles will be ruined—"

We see them on their muddy way

Where gum arabics splashing play—

Neat Petticoats thrown up on high,

Their drawers & ankles we descry—&c

THE FERRY AT FOUNTAIN'S STORE

*L*ocal residents measured time by remarkable happenings along the creek: the explosion of 1818, Lafayette's visit in 1825, the monstrous ice dam of 1827. Among such events, the freshet of 1822 was long remembered on the shores of the Tancopanican. To twelve-year-old Sophie it was "a great curiosity" and a personal disappointment:

> *Our bath house is gone and I am afraid Boyd will not make us another.* [S to H, 27 February 1822]

To Papa and Vic, returning from Philadelphia, it was a more serious matter:

> *We heard there had been a dreadful fresh in the Brandywine & that the bridge near Wilmington had been swept off. . . . there was no possibility of crossing over that night, the creek still being high, and the boat having been laid up for safety behind Fountain's store. You cannot form to yourself an idea of the height of the Brandywine on this occasion, it exceeds anything that ever happened before, the water came up into the piazza of the store, and on the other side it covered the gardens of my uncle's workmen.* [V to E, 24 February 1822]

Floods and storms were not the only causes of interruptions in ferry service. Sometimes Uncle Victor's workmen were the source of disruption.

Notice

Whereas Victor & Ch^s Dupont & Co. cloth manufacturers, in Brandywine hundred, county of New Castle State of Delaware, have through their attorney or attorneys and under pretence of caulking, mending & repairing their old flatboat, borrowed from Eleuthère Irénée Dupont Esqr. or from his attorney or attorneys another flat boat to use it as was said for three days, while their own flat boat should be caulked, mended or repaired, and through the laziness or drunkeness (perhaps both) of V & Ch Dupont's carpenter, or through any other cause, the aforesaid flat boat, belonging to said V & Ch Dupont, is lying still in an unfinished condition, & the aforesaid flat boat belonging to said E. I. Dupont Esqr is knocked about by drunken weavers, or left adrift among rocks and waterfalls.

["The Tancopanican Chronicle," 27 November 1824]

Apparently the crisis was quickly resolved, since a brief item under "Ship News" in the same issue announced that "the Ferry boat plying between Louviers and Eleutherian Mills has just been re-launched."

[*V°*]   *Crossing at the Ferry*

[*V°*]   *Fountain's modesty*

Normally, crossing the creek was routine for the inhabs, or homers, at Eleutherian Mills and the over-creekers at Louviers. Flatboats on either side of the creek plied back and forth as needed along a rope strung across the Brandywine. The flatboat was more than a ferry. For a moonlight excursion up the creek it was a pleasure craft.

> *The large boat had been prepared for the occasion. 6 chairs were arranged opposite to each other and we carried with us provisions. Our party was extremely pleasant and we returned about 9 o'clock. . . . afterwards we sat an hour in the Bower. Papa made us all sing for him notwithstanding Julia's repeated declaration that there was nothing worse for the voice than to sing at night in the open air.* [E to V, 30 June 1822]

Following the injury to her knee, Sophie found comfort as well as pleasure in a chair on the ferryboat. Without it she could not have visited Cousin Ella on her birthday.

> *Ella had set her heart on my going there that day—Accordingly, I was conveyed in the gig down to the boat, which was prepared, with a seat, for my reception. . . . I spent a most delightful day, and returned in the evening the same way as I went.* [S to H, 11 June 1827]

Not all crossings were so uneventful. A young lady could end up in the water (Cousin Julia stood by helplessly while neighbor Elizabeth McCall was rescued by a gardener who could not swim). Sophie reported a perilous passage in the company of two weavers en route to the woolen mill:

> *When I reached the shore, the boat was half way over, but two men who impelled it, <u>gallantly</u> came back for me—It was not till we had pushed off from shore some way, that I perceived the boat was freighted, (besides the two bipeds above mentioned) with a wheelbarrow, & a barrel; the latter containing some dark liquid, which was rapidly oozing between every stave, & meandering thro' the bottom of the boat—Imagining 'twas <u>soft soap</u>, I retreated from the rising surge on the edge of the boat, casting a look of horror on it, which did not escape one of my companions, a wretch hideous enough to represent Charon—"Hey, we've met with a misfortune here" croaked he, "our barrel's <u>stove in</u>"—"What is it, what is that?" said I, alarmed at the increasing waves that threatened to invade my still retreating steps—"Why sure its -----" explained the monster with a ferocious grin, naming a most horrible ingredient used in fulling cloth—I stood in perfect despair, when <u>Charon</u> wishing to make a graceful evolution, lost his*

balance, & went splash into the bottom of the boat! His hat & cane, set flying by the shock of his descent, went over board & alighted in a watery bed. The man rose enraged, & using language it chilled me to hear, insisted on his companion pushing back to try & recover the hat—but tho' he complied, the hat was gone too far along the tide to be reached, & the said companion perceiving my anxiety to part company, declared he must take the boat over, which he accordingly achieved, & I effected a landing, without further mischance, I had a good laugh with Ella over the affair. [S to H, 20 September 1832]

The hazards of crossing by ferry were encountered by visitors as well as inhabs. The August exodus from Philadelphia to escape the heat and the yellow fever brought many acquaintances to the nearby spa springs.

I have just now been interrupted by the appearance of a stage at our door, loaded with ladies! You may imagine the conversation which ensued—Sprol rushed to inspect its contents & parley with them, Vic flew after, having discovered 'twas the lady Grelaud, who is staying at the springs—She soon landed, accompanied by 7 of her scholars!! We peeped at them thro' the shutters, when Eleuthera discovering among them Miss Benjamina Price of Alexandria, an acquaintance of ours, & whose sister Mrs Mason nous a fait beaucoup de politesses, she had to fly & dress and appear, & what is worse, to escort them over the creek, whither the whole troop have gone to pay my aunt a visit.

[S to H, 23 August 1832]

According to an account in "The Tancopanican Chronicle" that same day, Mme. Grelaud was terrified of the river crossing. She

evinced her agitation by getting every moment nearer to the end of the boat: as she went backwards she did not see that she was gradually pushing Miss E. du Pont in the creek: Fortunately the stream was crossed ere the catastrophe could take place—

She had to be reassured that Cousin Frank, a naval officer, was capable of guiding the boat to safe harbor.

Comings and goings at the ferry ensured a steady flow of customers for Andrew Fountain, Esq., storekeeper, entrepreneur, and inveterate optimist, ever confident that the lost would be found. Though the du Pont daughters looked down their noses at "the old grey possum," deplored his choice of fashions, and made fun of his limited inventory, they incurred frequent charges in the account book at his emporium. Where else could

A new plan of crossing the creek.—

Scene 3.

Kicking the Ice.
Winter amusements on the opposite
shore of the Tancopanican—

Scene on the opposite shore—

The other day Lina came to Meta's on her little palfrey—Brother who was accustomed to Annette's standing stock still as long as he pleased, after he had taken Lina off, took off the saddle & left Miss Fountain standing by the door; but while he went to put away the saddle, away flew the beast—Brother rushed after her, Daniel Minney & another joined the chase, but she rushed down through the powder yard to the creek, swam it, & rolled herself in the mud by Tranchants—one of the men however, crossed over & caught her, & brought her back [S to H, 18 February 1832]

Scene 3ᵈ – The Store –

1 Mr Fountain did I leave my handkerchief here?

2 No Miss I did not see it

3 Stop, I seed one here – here 'tis

2 Take that away thats not it

1 No sir   mine was a white one –

4 Hahahaha!

(1,4, in front of the store laughing)

[V°]   The Emporium

1st Sophie. "Mr Fountain, will you let me
look at your sewing silk?"

2^d Mr Fountain (Handing down a pile of
bombazets) "Yes Ma'am,
here's all we have" –

New Fall Goods. –

Messrs. A Fountain & Co. respectfully inform their friends and the public that they have just received an assortment
of the best and most fashionable fall goods among which are Rob Roy calicoes, elegant chester Jaconet, Superior
calicoes of all colours, Superfine Bombazines, Children's spats and Fleecy gloves also Ten fashionable mustard pots
in the shape of Egyptian mummies, small black pitchers, innumerable tea pots, Salt fish, boiled cinnamon, rancid
butter and an elegant assortment of Merino shawls which they will dispose of on the most reasonable terms and
unlimited credit. – ["The Tancopanican Chronicle," Novr 27th 1824]

Eleu, on short notice, obtain spices for her walnut pickles? Where else could Sophie find her dress silks? Or mousetraps? And, when a replacement was needed for sister Lina's little donkey, Annette, it was the store-keeper who provided a new mount. However ridiculous he might appear, Andrew Fountain was a man of some importance. His store was a gathering place, a minor landmark where household provisioning could be combined with creek crossings.

> *The creek is still frozen over strong enough for persons to cross on it—On Thursday, being the only tolerable day we've had yet, Meta, Mary, Eliza, Eleu and I went over the creek—we crossed on the ice above the dam, & came home by the boat. Alfred was fortunately with us, for we had some difficulty in landing owing to the ice on the edge—We went to the store, as we wanted something—Meta entering, stumbled up against something, she raised her eyes up, up, up till at last nearly at the ceiling she encountered, Great Gibbon's astonished phiz—she burst out alaughing and to conceal it turned to the counter, when she beheld little Fountain, with a green cotton handkerchief tied over his eyes, surmounted by a blue woollen cap, tipped with a scarlet tassel! You may think this did serve to restore her equanimity. We were roaring so, we had to stand some time at the door.* [S to H, 6 February 1830]

Fountainic mishaps made entertaining reading in the pages of "The Tancopanican Chronicle" on October 18, 1823:

> *Messrs. Editors, . . . I hope you will insert in your columns the following circumstance, which happened lately to Mr Fountain; of the firm of A Fountain & co, at his wharehouse, and fancy store, opposite to the ferry. . . . One evening, he received three dozen eggs, which were particularly welcome; eggs, having been for some time, rather scarce. He therefore put them away carefully in a basket, under a shelf. Early the next morning, a customer asked for eggs. The Boy, (delighted at not having to answer, "None at present, but we expect some to morrow") hastily went to the place where the eggs were deposited; but, lo! they had disappeared. Mr Fountain was summoned . . . he began to make a shrewd guess, and to smell a <u>rat</u>. The store was searched from the attics to the vaults; when in the cellar, near a heap of rubbish, the shell of an egg was found; upon removing the said rubbish, the thirty five remaining eggs were seen, piled up with great ingenuity by these industrious creatures; and, strange to tell, none of the eggs cracked though these animals had to descend a flight of steps, with their brittle prize. Whether the spirit of imitation seized upon these rats, and made them wish to have a <u>Store</u> of their own, for moments of necessity, or*

scarcity, is not known; but certainly this instance of perseverance, and adroitness, in these animals deserves to be recorded; as well as the tenderness of heart, of Mr A. Fountain; who was so touched by the pathos of the "rats petition," that he permits them ever since to flourish unmolested in his store. —Philomus-rat

During a business trip with Papa to West Chester, Pennsylvania, Sophie and Eleu were "gallanted" about town by Fountain. The "old grey possum" happened to be there also on business.

Papa invited him to join us on an excursion on the West Chester railroad—He accordingly escorted us to the house where the car is kept, But when we arrived there we found that there was no horse, & that they would not put the car in motion till 2 oclock which would be too late for us—so we proceeded to walk round the town—The big Grey Possum accompanied us, acting beau, it was enough to make one roar to see his grinning phiz, distended by his efforts to apear charming, his consequential airs, & amiable speeches—I assure you Eleu & I had some difficulty in suppressing our smiles—He dined with us at the hotel, & after dinner we lost sight of the Possum to our great satisfaction. [S to H, 18 July 1832]

Despite her glee at parting company for the moment with Mr. Fountain, Sophie expressed sincere regret when it was rumored that he was to leave the Brandywine forever. Long after his departure, Sophie's expressive language recalled his presence. When a misplaced letter or an article from her sewing basket "adopted invisibility," she bore it with "Fountainic philosophy, being well assured 'twill come to light—'twill reappear."

It will come to light.

THE PRIMER CLASS

*S*ophie had cherished for years a secret yearning to be, like Henry, a West Point cadet. Sensitive to the differences in the education of men and women, she was annoyed when Henry referred to his engineering textbook drawings as "lithographic absurdities."

> *How can you speak so, of the very things you went to West Point to learn—You know you did not go there, to learn to march or drill; or merely to say, you had been there; but to acquire a knowledge of many of the most useful as well as interesting sciences, which are no where else in this country so well taught—I should be too happy, girl as I am, if I had the opportunities you have, Harry; & I should find much pleasure in the very studies you seem to despise—Do not think these subjects a matter of indifference to me; tho' a woman & therefore having other duties & employments to take up my time. The <u>lithographic absurdities</u> you mention I should particularly like to study.*
>
> [S to H, 5 December 1831]

It was all the more frustrating that Papa was aware of her longings and her capacities. She recorded his words:

> *"Je voudrais bien que ce fut toi que j'ai envoyé a West Point!" Oh how often has this been my wish! for I feel within me the strength, the energy, that <u>would</u> have borne me thro' the fearful ordeal.* [DIARY, February 1833]

But Sophie's ordeal was four months at Mrs. Grimshaw's. Within weeks of her return, her brief formal schooling completed, she was eager to assume the responsibility for a class of her own at the Brandywine Manufacturers' Sunday School, a pleasant walk from home in good weather. She was given the littlest girls to teach, the primer class, in the fall of 1825, just before her fifteenth birthday. Sophie was devoted to them.

> *On Sunday we went to school as usual. There were a great many children there, 175, I believe—and we were a little short of Teachers, Ella having gone to New Castle—You cannot think what an interest I take in many of those children, particularly <u>my</u> class. There are a good many new scholars that came while I was in Phil*[a]*—Among others, a little girl of <u>three</u> years old, who already reads quite fluently such sentences as "My ox is fat"—She is one of the prettiest youngies I ever saw, and very well behaved—I am quite busy now arranging premiums for my class—*
>
> [S to H, 25 March 1828]

The monthly rewards, or premiums, for perfect attendance included the usual small books of moral tales

The Primer class at S. School

[*V°*] *Teacher – Miss Sophie*

Scholars – Mary Kyle, Elisa Jane Flemming, Elisa Jane Armstrong,

Margaret Fineghan, Elisa Jane Reed, Sarah Reed

I thought of you and Joan on Sunday morning, as Mary and I were proceeding to Sunday School; you were probably at that time similarly engaged–I found four new scholars in my class at school; they appear interesting little girls. . . . Elisa and Sarah Reed, the little girls of whom I spoke to you are to leave our place on Wednesday–They both appeared much grieved at leaving Sunday School, I assure you I was not less so, to see them go. . . .

[S to Clementina Smith, 16 April 1832]

and religious tracts, but most prized by the fortunate candidates were the lovingly hand-stitched items prepared by their teachers. Admiring the penwipers, thread cases, and pincushions one Premium Sunday, Alfred was so charmed by the "noble" size of a particular pincushion that he insisted on its being presented to him. But Vic was unrelenting; such efforts were intended only for scholars.

The Sunday School convened every Sabbath morning. Promptly at half after eight teachers Vic, Tat, and Sophie, and sometimes Alfred and Alexis, were at their posts, unless delayed by an untimely visit from John Phillips or Vic's last-minute feeding of her birds. In bad weather they sometimes reached school after a "joltation" in the two-wheeled powder cart (used for carrying pigs as well as powder). Uncle Charles had suggested the cart one rainy morning when Vic, Tat, Alexis, and a classmate from Mr. Bullock's school could not all fit in the open gig. To the boys the cart was a great adventure, and Vic preferred it because it was canvas-covered. Sophie disliked it intensely because it gave her a headache.

> *On Sunday we had the pleasure of a ride to School in the powder cart—Breakneck hill, (that hill near <u>Pigpen</u> row, or <u>Middletown</u> as its inhabs call it) is worse than ever, so that we had an <u>inexpressibly jolty</u> ride of it—I prefered wading home thro' <u>Swampfoot</u> lane (the lane between Meta's and Lina's) & let the others ride in the vehicle.*
>
> [S to H, 18 February 1832]

Hurra! Eliza run!

Mr & Mrs Hogg arrived yesterday in their barouche from the family mansion <u>Pig stye Hall</u> New Castle, and are for the present located at Hagley the seat of James A Bidermann Esqr where we are informed it is their intention to spend some time. ["The Tancopanican Chronicle," Nov[r] 27th 1824]

The Missionary's Visit

Yesterday being such a beautiful day, I went to SSchool and after school went and dined at Linas, because Mr. Love was to preach in the afternoon and I wished to go and hear him. Accordingly, Pol and I went, and fortunately early, for if we had not, we never would have got seats. . . . I never saw that school house half so full—There was actually no room for the people—Mr. Love gave us a very long sermon, and it was night when church let out—

[S to H, 3 December 1827]

Ella staid here for dinner and went to church with us and fell quite in Love with his reverence who, to do him justice gave us a very good sermon but only think of the horrors after we had arisen to go out Mr Love, after giving out about the communion that is to take place next sunday says "I am appointed by the missionary society of New Castle to preach here every two sundays for three months" and then he added if there were no objections to the use of the house. it was well he added that for Mrs Bauduy was furious and Sophia was very much alarmed at the idea of her addressing him in full congregation. however she contented herself with telling him that it would be too great an interruption to the Harmonie. he seemed a little hurt I thought [Polly Simmons to E, 3 May 1828]

Side by side, at weekly morning sessions, Quaker, Catholic, Presbyterian, Methodist, and Episcopalian children learned to read and write, then recited their catechisms. Until the first public school opened, in 1831, the Sunday School and the night classes conducted across the creek by Mr. Gibbon were the only sources of formal education for offspring of local farmers and millworkers. "Great" Gibbon, a man of unusual height, whose unruly shock of hair made him seem gigantic, also taught in the Sunday School. He was holding forth on one of those mornings when the arrival of the du Pont ladies was delayed by cold weather. Sophie described the scene:

the Pleasures of S School

1	2	3	4	5
At nine or more	*The sound that flows*	*Then in we bounce*	*The teachers next*	*We see him stand*
We reach the door	*Forth thro his nose*	*All four at once*	*Are quite perplexed*	*A pen in hand–*
Half frozen thro'	*Salutes our ear–*	*And off we haul*	*When they're inclined*	*This first he mends,*
And tired too,	*Incensed we hear*	*Our Cloaks & shawl*	*To write and find*	*To us extends,*
Then we espy	*For at the door*	*(Our hats are hung*	*The pens all split,*	*When lo, what shrieks*
Perch'd up on high	*An hour or more*	*The boys among,*	*Or stumps unfit–*	*What howls! What squeeks,*
With book in hand	*We're doom'd to wait*	*For on our side*	*. . . .*	*On slate it makes.*
Great Gibbon stand	*Till Gibbon Great*	*No room is spied)*	*While thus stand we*	*The stillness breaks!*
	At the last clause,	*. . . .*	*With joy we see*	*The babies all*
	Shall make a pause		*From t'other side*	*Begin to bawl,*
			Great Gibbon stride	*While puppies nine*
			With hair upright	*In chorus join–*
			A foot in height–	*Our lips we bite,*
				Lest we outright
				Should laugh or grin,
				Amid the din–

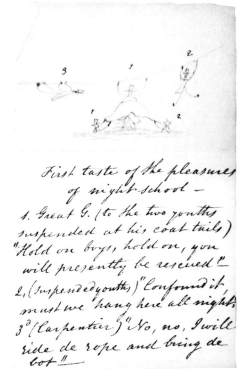

First taste of the pleasures of night-school –
1. Great G. (to the two youths suspended at his coat tails) "Hold on boys, hold on, you will presently be rescued." 2, (suspended youths) "Confound it, must we hang here all night. 3°(Carpentier) "No, no, I will ride de rope and bring de bot."

Night School

I must tell you a good adventure of great Gibbons, which I heard today – You must know he has taken under his supreme control the wits of the overcreeker youths, formerly the pupils of the learned and accomplished Jonathan and Walcott. For this purpose he goes over the creek every evening. [S to H, 23 October 1829]

First taste of the pleasures of night school–

The other night, at about 10 oclock, he (Gibbon), and Carpentier (who had accompanied him over) and who, the story says, was half asleep from the effects of night school), and three youths, came to the creek, when lo! they found the boat was on this side. They took the little trough boat, (with which I believe you are acquainted) and all five got in. Suddenly, the chain broke, they all rushed to one end of the boat to catch the rope—when lo! in dipt the boat, and gliding from beneath their feet immersed them in the crystal wave—Gibbon, Carpentier, and a third had hold of the rope, the other two I presume held on by Gibbons coat tails—Carpentier, who is nimble, mounted the rope, and climbing along it in true monkey style, reached our shore, got the boat, and went to his companions' rescue. They were wet up the neck, and in this dripping state they had to make the best of their way home.

[S to H, 23 October 1829]

In time Sophie gained a sense of self-confidence.

I have had a good deal of experience in the <u>teaching</u> line since <u>six years</u> that I have a class at Sunday School, and I know that it requires we should exert no little dominion over ourselves, to be always calm, mild, and patient in such an office. [S to H, 20 September 1831]

Paramount among the demands she made on herself were regular home visits—"pastorals" she called them—to all her girls, despite the many obstacles of time and terrain, and her natural timidity. Crossing the wire bridge to visit a pupil ill with consumption was a frightening ordeal for Sophie, though Vic kindly accompanied her and led the way, allaying her fears but not the dizziness that overcame her. She felt reluctant to intrude upon the families of her scholars, particularly on Saturday afternoons when "the mothers are cleaning up house, the fathers coming in dirty from the mills, to wash etc." And her status as a single young woman with a keenly developed sense of propriety sometimes presented a dilemma, as in the case of a favorite scholar, Mary Donnan, daughter of the local tavern keeper.

The girls all knew references but M. Donnan. . . . she said she had lost the book this week—I will endeavor to go & see her this week—But it is very hard to do so, as I don't think it would be proper for me to go into the tavern, as I don't know what scenes I might not fall into—but how otherwise to see her I can't tell. [DIARY, 4 March 1832]

Sophie did at least have the consolation of friends who shared and understood her frustrations.

Do not you find the presence of the mothers of the scholars at times a great difficulty? Most of them, I have found, talk so incessantly that I can scarcely say a word to the children—& they seem to think the best thing they can do, is to praise their childrens <u>smartness</u> at learning, . . . that we only care for their proficiency in reading & spelling, though I always try to explain to them that our chief desire is that the children should understand & practice at home what they learn on Sunday. Do tell me if you meet with the same difficulties in the mothers of your scholars? [S to Clementina Smith, 26 June 1832]

So devoted was Sophie to her primer class—and the girls to their teacher—that promotions were postponed for several years.

Are not these promotions <u>trying</u> things? Two of the girls whom I am to lose this quarter (Anne & Margaret Aiken, I think you know them?) have been in my class ever since I first taught it, which is now <u>seven years!</u> I cannot bear the idea of parting with them, I am much attached to them & I believe they are to me. Indeed it is natural that habit should render them so, having never had another teacher and it was their reluctance to being promoted which has occasioned their remaining so long with me. But now I believe it to be my duty to give them up, tho' it is a painful one . . . . I am sure most persons would laugh at me, if they knew my expressing so much regret & concern about two little girls . . . . [S to Clementina Smith, 26 June 1832]

No matter how comfortable or how competent Sophie became with her own little girls, she continued to be plagued by the annoying shyness that made her so self-conscious, especially with the teachers of the boys' classes.

When I came in to school, Mr Hoskins was by the door, unmuffling, We exchanged bows—I <u>ought</u> to have gone up & told him I was glad of his recovery. . . . Oh that I could correct myself of this awkward bashfulness, which is ridiculous in a person of my age; it makes me unhappy & uncomfortable, for it prevents my doing to others those civilities which duty <u>requires</u> as I have deeply felt today— [DIARY, 19 February 1832]

But her most awkwardly anxious moment was occasioned by a visit from Papa to the Sunday School. It was unusual for Papa, with his deist convictions, to attend.

He sat there while Mr. H[oskins] closed school—I felt a great dread that dear Papa should disapprove of the manner in which this was done—My head throbbed & my knees trembled, as we rose for the prayer, & I breathed one, that he might not be led away by any prejudice to think what was done amiss—So far my prayer has been heard, he has said nothing of it— [DIARY, 1831]

Sophie respected Papa's beliefs, but in religious matters she followed the dictates of her own heart, for herself and for others. Teaching in the Sunday School was

not a <u>task</u>, but a pleasure, because we take so much interest in it—And so indeed must everyone who reflects how much is placed in the power of a S. School teacher— [S to H, 18 October 1830]

PERAMBULATIONS

*A*ll Philadelphia was in a whirlwind of preparations for the coming visit of the Marquis de Lafayette, and Sophie was there. She had gone up to town with her sisters, who were invited to attend the welcoming festivities and the grand ball in his honor. Sophie, at fourteen, was considered too young to be included in all the social functions but seemed content to watch all the fuss going on around her. Victorine remarked,

> *It is impossible to be more kind and attentive than Mrs. Smith is to our girls, especially to our little sensitive plant Sophie who I believe enjoys herself as much as she possibly can away from home.* [v to Ev, September 1824]

Actually Sophie's presence in Philadelphia served a practical purpose. She and Vic took the opportunity to visit several schools. Vic knew the time had come to send Sophie away, "to wean her from home," to help her overcome her timidity. It was just four months after this Philadelphia visit that Sophie entered Mrs. Grimshaw's school, where she was painfully homesick. Her tears were of no avail, though, so she was sensible enough to learn to tolerate Mrs. Grimshaw's mischievous children and Mrs. Grimshaw's monstrous cat.

> *How happy should I be dear Henry, if there were here any girl of my own disposition, who was fond of collections and scientific pursuits—I am more disgusted with school than ever—If I was at school at Mrs Fret[ageot]s or some place in the country I would be so much happier—* [s to H, 11 May 1825]

Academically Sophie surpassed most of her classmates; in fact her sole challenge proved to be her twice-a-week drawing lessons with Mr. Lesueur. A series of caricatures about school life, a lifelong friend in the person of classmate Mary Black, and new experience in drawing were the tangible gains from four months of misery away from her beloved Brandywine.

During those spring months Sophie was well aware of the kindness of family friends in Philadelphia, like the Smiths and the Lammots. Cotton manufacturer Daniel Lammot was Papa's good friend. Anna Potts Smith Lammot, his second wife, had been a classmate of sister Vic's years before. When she was overburdened with infants and adolescent stepchildren, Victorine journeyed up to help with the babies, and Meta, her eldest stepdaughter, welcomed the young Lammots for visits at Nemours. Sophie adopted Mary Augusta Lammot as her first close friend outside her family, even dedicating to her "One Day on the Tancopanican" (the earliest surviving booklet of carics). When courtship diverted Mary from her Brandywine friend, her younger sister Elenora replaced her as Sophie's cohort in summertime mischief. Nevertheless, in November 1832 Sophie served as Mary's first bridesmaid and then accompanied the newlyweds to Philadelphia, where she spent several weeks with them in their new home.

The Smiths lived in adjacent houses on Lombard Street in Philadelphia. Francis Gurney Smith was Papa's Philadelphia agent as well as his close friend; two of his children, Tom and Joanna, eventually married du Ponts. The association dated back to the War of 1812, and brother Richard S. Smith's friendship with the du Ponts was of equally long standing. Visits to one Smith family invariably entailed visits next door. When Henry was sick with the mumps at the G. Smith's, for example, Sophie was delighted to visit the R. Smiths next door as well. She wrote to Henry:

I cannot tell which I love most, of the two families—I think I love them equally. [December 1830]

Sophie's closest friend in the R. Smith family was Clementina, some four years younger. "Clem" appears in but one of Sophie's drawings, but their attachment grew stronger over the years. Sophie deeply admired her firm self-discipline and her obedience, traits that she sought to strengthen in herself:

I never knew so industrious & persevering a little creature as Clementina. . . . as soon as tea is over, no matter what temptation she may have to remain in the parlour, she would go up stairs & study her lessons till bed time; And in the morning, long before day, the first sounds I heard on waking, were those of dear Clem's harp—How few girls of sixteen, beautiful and agreeable as she is, & possessing so many inducements for mingling in society, would act as she does. [S to H, 1 December 1830]

Late in 1831 the R. Smiths became neighbors of the Lammots at Lenni, the Rockdale milling community on Chester Creek. Although Lenni was but twelve miles distant from Eleutherian Mills, it was not always easy to find a means of transport.

Yesterday morning Eleuthera & I set off for Lenni. We went over the creek, & took Charles' dearborne, a little before 8. We had a lovely ride over there, our steeds went like the wind. All the people we met <u>stared</u> as usual, tho' not quite so much as they did at <u>your uniform</u>. We met several waggoners most of whom would not move out of their way in *the least to give us the road, & one of them being <u>politely</u> requested to do so by Joliecoeur exclaimed, "Why don't you get out of the way yourself with your <u>load of hay</u>." The idea of calling two fair damsels a load of <u>Hay</u>! We were indignant, so was our ecuyer, who exclaimed to the next <u>savages</u> we met "Why, what sort of people are you, in this part of the country!"* [S to H, 6 August 1831]

Sophie's first trip to Lenni, the year before, had taken about three hours:

The ride <u>is</u> a long one, but not unpleasant, and as you approach nearer to Lenni, many parts of the road are beautiful. It was just about sunset, when we stopped at Mr Lammots gate, and no one perceived us coming, for the road is so situated that you cannot be seen till you reach the gate, & even <u>then</u>, only in case a person is stationed at the parlour window. We entered the house & walked into the parlour, without their having any idea of our presence– . . . such <u>yelling</u> you never heard, Elenora came rushing in, & it was quite a scene– . . . . We took long walks every fine day, Elenor, Mary & I; but Mrs L. always would send the children with us, which was a great annoyance, as I never knew so detestable a set of brats in my life. . . . There are wild hills, covered with woods & rocks, it looks lovely. . . . I never saw so many wildflowers anywhere as there are there, for the cattle never have access to these woods, so that the anemonies violets & buttercups &c &c make quite a <u>carpet</u> under the lofty trees & bushes, while the height of the hills & profusion of large rocks give the whole a most romantic air. [S to H, 17 April 1830]

Through the Lammots another young lady was introduced into Sophie's growing circle of friends. They had come to know Eliza Schlatter because of their mutual affiliation with the Swedenborgian Church of the New Jerusalem. Eliza came from Germantown, where she lived near the roadside in "a neat little cottage, with trees around it, & an orchard behind–" Sophie especially enjoyed her first trip to Eliza's because the carriage en route passed by Mt. Airy College, Henry's alma mater. She returned to Philadelphia for a busy round of excursions that included her first visit to Bartram's Garden and an expedition to Fairmount Park,

which, as 'twas the first of May, was alive with large parties of children & young people, loaded with flowers– Fairmount has been greatly improved lately, to a beautiful spot– We then went to the porcelain factory, It was very amusing & curious to see the porcelain made—Some of the specimens are beautiful, I had no idea they could do so well in this country. We had a delightful ride out to the garden, which we found beautiful, as it contains a great

General Jackson is a great military character. He will do very well in a Subordinate station—but I should not like to see him head. Our country is already a great deal too military—

(Spoken through his nose)

We dined at Chester and stopped again at Darby where we saw a quaker original, inveighing against Jackson. I have drawn a picture of him and intend sending it brother Bidermann. . . . Directions for painting the caricature—coat—quaker color, pantaloons the same, stockings blue—boots Black—Hat dirty black, light black eyes—waistcoat light quaker colour. I wish I could have had an Indian rubber I should have drawn it much better. [S to E, 15 February 1825]

quantity of our own native flowers—Many of them were in bloom. . . . Were you ever at Gray's Ferry? We passed by there, & what a sweet place it is! [S to H, 3 May 1830]

The Smiths saw to it that Sophie was introduced to most of the attractions of the city. Her first trip to the theater was to see the celebrated Miss Clara Fisher.

I was rather disappointed. The play I saw was Douglas—Clara Fisher acted the part of young Norval; every one said she acted it badly—and indeed, I dont see how it could be otherwise—For she is a very small woman, and in man's dress did not look larger than James—and you can conceive how ridiculous it appeared to see such a little fellow, fighting with Glenalbin and exciting the jealousy of Lord Randolph &c. . . . I felt an almost irresistible inclination to laugh. . . . After all, I do not see how people can be so very fond of the theatre—But I ought not to judge after going only once. [S to Ev, 20 March 1828]

Despite the efforts of her friends, Sophie was still beset with homesickness when she was in town:

dear sisters, do forgive me if I have inadvertently dissatisfied you—If my letters were stupid last week, 'tis I had little leisure, & felt stupid myself— & if they were sometimes dull, 'tis that I thought of home— . . . I had various slight attacks of home sickness—but they are quite cured now, particularly since I've heard of your indignation, & I think how often I'd be called "little goose" were I with you— [S to E, 12 November 1832]

A Rainy day,
No 267 South Front Street

March 11–1828
Tuesday afternoon–

Scene (Seen?) in a gale

Lady in accents of despair,
"Oh shocking!" !!!!!!!!

Fashions for November

Quaker Meeting

Alexandria
31st May

Tuesday afternoon

Poor absolution for
the loss of the Society
of our friends!—

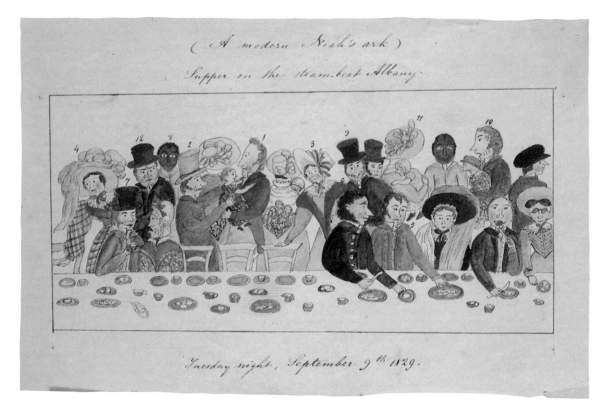

Supper on the steamboat Albany (A modern Noah's ark)

We went down early in order to get seats, and took ones near the wall next Mrs. Kemble. . . . then commenced a scene, which can neither be imagined nor described, but must have been seen, felt, and smelt, ere one can form an idea of its discomfort & singularity. We were 500 on board, the majority women and children, and as many were stowed in the cabin as it could inconveniently contain. All who were nearest the tables, seated themselves first to supper. the rest remained in a kind of moving chaos, some standing, some sitting, and all talking. The mingled exclamations of wrath, pleasantry, and terror, the laughing of the gentlemen, The groans of the ladies, the squaling of the babies, the rattling of teacups, plates, and knives, assailed the ear with a hideous din – while our sense of smelling was no less molested by the perfume of salt fish, peppermint, fried ham, and other nameless odours as various as disgusting – To complete the whole, the windows were all closed and the air suffocating –
Miss Boleman at last effected the opening of a window behind us, which gave us much relief; I amused myself for some minutes with the odd sight before me, a sketch of which I have since committed to paper and will perhaps send you a copy for yr amusement. [S to H, 11 September 1829]

In the same letter Sophie reported on the errands assigned to her by her sisters on the Brandywine:

I asked Joan to come with me & we went to ask about the chintz at Days, it is not a y^d wide, but the usual calico width—all the chintzes are that width & price, but such large & bright figures! I'll enclose you a pattern of Clem's dress, which if you like better, I can get ours like it—Every thing is in bedquilt style now—I went to Bessons, Faucetts, & other places, & these remarks are the result of my inquiries—

She was careful to oblige with details concerning her trips to the American Sunday School Union for the books Vic sought; her shoe-shopping forays, when boots in the shop window made her think the store handled men's shoes and therefore she could not properly enter; what outfits were conspicuous on Chestnut Street. She avoided offering her opinions.

On later trips, in writing to Frank, she was more open:

I was quite delighted to exchange the monotony of the steamboat for the stage, tho' it was rather a jolty one— I've come to the conclusion that railroads are the most disagreable means of travelling, & stages the most agreeable. Steamboats come between the two, convenience in a great measure compensating for ennui—

[S to SFDP, 23 April 1833]

Her assessment was by then based on considerable experience. In 1829 she had gone with Papa, Vic, Brother, and Lil to visit Henry at West Point, then, with stops in New York, to investigate schools in New Haven and Lawrenceville, New Jersey, before returning home. On that trip almost everything had been new to Sophie, who had not previously traveled beyond Philadelphia. She was most thrilled with West Point, but she thoroughly enjoyed seeing the mineral collection at Yale and visiting a Sunday School in Trenton. She drew carics all along the way (only two have survived).

She also journeyed several times to Alexandria to visit the Cazenoves. The du Pont–Cazenove friendship dated back to 1788, when Uncle Victor first came to America. It had been strengthened over the years by Papa's business dealings with Mr. Cazenove, and by school experiences shared by both sons and daughters. Because of the difficulties of travel between Philadelphia and Alexandria, the young Cazenoves frequently visited on the Brandywine during their school vacations. "You see that, one after the other my children are overjoyed to

Steam boat scene—

O I pray I implore you!

The captain! stop the boat! O my bagage! my band boxes!

Scene 4ᵗʰ   The Shoemaker

1   Mᵣ Henderson my shoes are so immense I cant wear them

2   Ma'am does she mean they are too large or too small?

Costumes & Customs in Alexandria

[*V°*] *1st Gent —Well how do you do—This has been a very hot day—*
2nd Gent—Indeed it has—I can scarcely endure this weight of vesture

Little urchin (speaking to himself) Well, I dare say her feet
  have had a good washing now if they have not had one
  for a month   ha, ha, ha!!

Lady (in accents of affright) Oh, take care boy, this is
  rather <u>too</u> cooling (to herself) I never knew anything
  <u>quite</u> equal the impertinence of these children

accept your kind invitation to spend their vacations with you," wrote Antoine Charles Cazenove to Irénée du Pont, on September 9, 1817. Reciprocally, the du Pont girls spent time in Alexandria. A number of Sophie's caricatures were drawn there, while she was visiting Charlotte Cazenove, her friend Lotta, whose early death, in 1836, following the birth of her only child, caused Sophie to write in her diary, "the strongest most cherished tie of friendship that had bound my heart was broken." Measured in years, their friendship was brief, but it was intense, with Lotta serving as Sophie's bridesmaid in 1833.

Tat was bridesmaid for Lotta's sister Paulina in 1831. Sophie also traveled to Alexandria for the wedding, some weeks ahead of Tat. Caught up in the prenuptial festivities, she had little time for the usual bouts of homesickness. The Cazenoves saw to it that Sophie went to Mount Vernon, the Falls of the Potomac, and Washington, D.C. In the city, she stayed with Mrs. Cazenove's sister, Mrs. Archibald Henderson, wife of the first Marine Corps commandant.

> *I do like to stay at Mrs Hendersons very much. . . . She has a lovely large house & pretty yard, & nice little piazzas, on one of which were two pet guinea pigs, that I fell in love with—And then, one side of the house opens on to the little garden & this little garden on the* parade ground, *a* long *Green plain bordered with acacia trees (now in full bloom). On one side the parade ground is enclosed by a highwall, over which the U.S. flag waves all day, & on the other side are the barracks, looking so neat & pretty, they altogether form the* beau ideal *of military life—There are very few marines now at the Washington barracks—In the afternoon the band played twice, once for us, & then again for some visitors—this was truly delightful—And at night just as I was dropping asleep . . . we were roused by music again, & had a long & delightful serenade from the band—* [S to H, 13 May 1831]

With Lotta, Sophie toured the Capitol, where, as she wrote in the same letter to Henry, she longed to have more time in the Library of Congress.

> *It is a very handsome r[oom] & contains a great many books of splendid prints—We had not time t[o] stop & look at them, the only one I saw was a vol of a work on Entomology containing very handsome representations of the insects & the plants on which they feed—We are to pay another visit to Washington, & then I hope to go again to the library.*

[*V°*]   *Consolation*–
C. (On a chair contemplating herself in the glass)
Well–'tis a great comfort to be small–
For now I can have <u>any one</u>, but if I were six feet high,
none of the shorties would dare come near me–

Washington–*Attitude for barberizing*
Tuesday afternoon   June 21ˢᵗ 1831–

[*V°*]

Charlotte–*Hold up your head Sophy and look*–
        <u>like a man</u>
Sophia–*I have no such ambition*–*How Elu*
        would laugh if she saw our
        <u>attitude</u> for <u>hairdressing</u>–
        Something so novel–
Soph–*looking out the window, Ah! voila Monsieur le*
        Colonel coming down the road <u>already</u>
Charlotte looking–*Yes in the Shape of a <u>blackey</u>*–
        goes on with her operation–

[*V°*]   *Preparations for a tea fight*–
A new plan to look bright & put Morpheus to flight,
when you go out at night–
Washington   June 7 1831   Friday afternoon–

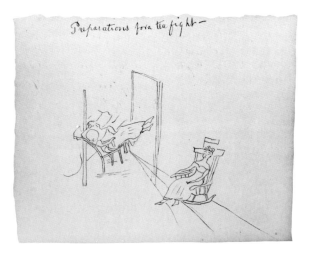

Sophie's letter included an enthusiastic account of a trip through the Navy Yard:

The next morning at nine we went down to the Navy Yard to see the Potomac, the vessel on which Irvine Shubrick is going out—He met us there, & kindly taking me under his care, showed me every thing & explained all to me—I had never before been on board a vessel of any kind—All was novelty, & very deeply interesting to me; I could not help thinking all the time, of Frank, cooped up in such a dark dismal place as it is—The captains quarters are very comfortable & large & cheerful looking, and the gun deck appears pleasant enough, but the midshipmen's and lieutenants abode is all gloom, & below these, 'tis perfect erebus—We visited the armoury, & also the place where they make the blocks for pulleys & other machinery of the ships; I was much pleased to see a circular saw, as I had not seen any before, & was surprized at the rapidity with which they cut—

To Tat, Sophie sent practical advice about the wardrobe she should bring for the wedding:

I advise you Tat, to have yourself a couple or so, of those little aprons, either of book muslin, or figured or squared muslin, or anything fanciful & small. For they are universally worn here & are very useful to save the dress. For we are so large a family & will be so much more so when you & Mr. Greenleaf are here, & Anne Henderson is staying at Mrs. Gardiners, that we never have tea on table, but it is handed round. And you know in a large merry laughing moving party things often get spilt. Besides these little aprons are very useful at all times to keep the front of frocks clean. I advise you to bring on a good supply of gloves they are worn here from sunrise till bedtime.

[S to E, 9 May 1831]

Of her hosts, Sophie wrote,

I do not think there ever was a merrier family in the world than this one, every soul of them appears happy & contented, nothing but joking & laughing going on all day & never a hasty word, not a murmur of discontent or vexation, from any member, grown up, or children. The only way in which it can be accounted for, is, because they are all so good. [S to H, 13 May 1831]

Yet even so, an "entre nous" told Henry,

When I thought of the pleasant circle round our own hearth at home, my heart was weary to be with them—

PORTRAITS FOR PAPA

*P*apa wanted all his daughters to be painted by artist Rembrandt Peale. The two eldest had sat for their portraits in the summer of 1813, soon after completing their studies at Mme. Rivardi's school in Philadelphia. For as long as Sophie could remember, their pictures had hung in the parlor at Eleutherian Mills. In both, the artist had clearly delineated the cleft chin that was an unmistakable du Pont characteristic. Now, almost two decades later, Mr. Peale would have the opportunity of capturing the two younger du Pont sisters on canvas.

> *On Saturday we heard that Mr. Peale was to be in Phil^a that day. I don't know if I ever wrote you that Papa had agreed with that gentleman that he should take Eleu's & my portrait this fall. We will of course both have to be in Philad^a for the purpose. . . . I shall only stay in town as long as 'tis necessary, to have my picture taken, which will be a week or ten days I expect. I do not wish to go up at this time much and don't like the thoughts of sitting for my picture, but we must often do what we don't like, & should try to make the best of every thing. . . . As I wanted several articles of dress for this visit which Vic considered me too inexperienced in the shopping line to procure, she determined to go up herself for two or three days & stay at Mrs. R Smith's.* [S to H, 1 November 1831]

Accordingly, Eleuthera went up to the city with Victorine, leaving Sophie to follow two weeks later. For the first time Sophie traveled without a companion, but her father consigned her to the care of the steamboat captain. On board she found several acquaintances, among them a Colonel McKenna, who had written an account of his tour among the Indians, one of her favorite subjects. So she was neither lonesome nor bored.

Sophie's estimate that her portrait would take a week to ten days was mistaken, for Peale was not to be rushed. She wrote to Henry how slow the artist was but how pleased she was that Papa had at last consented to have his portrait taken too, and that he had already had his first sitting.

Convinced that Peale could not be hurried, Sophie settled into the daily routine of bundling up and trudging from the Smiths' to the studio.

> *I have been three times to Mr. Peale. His room is in Market between 5th & 6th Sts. It is so long a walk I am tired out when I get home. I set 2 hours at a time & am wearied by it already. Though as Joan has always gone with me 'tis not very tiresome.* [S to H, 16 November 1831]

As the portrait progressed, Sophie and Joanna were joined by brother Richard Smith, who took a great interest in observing the artist at work. Evenings passed pleasantly, with Joanna singing to the accompaniment of Richard's guitar. Much as Sophie enjoyed their "musicales," she felt that Richard might not have been dismissed from West Point in the spring had he paid more attention to his studies and less to his guitar. Now that he was about to return to the Point for a second chance, Sophie sent an urgent plea to Henry to keep a watchful eye on Richard:

> *You, my dear brother, are, or should be, his best friend there. Independently of the personal interest I believe you feel in him, the great intimacy which exists between our family and his, seems to place you nearer to each other. Richard is a sweet-tempered, affectionate, and, I believe, sensible young man. If he should fail at West Point, I fear he would be ruined. The whole happiness of his life is at stake. Oh, that he could feel it so! I fear his fondness, his passion I might say, for music, will be his greatest snare.* [S to H, 7 December 1831]

November 29th 1831 – Walnut & fourth (fatal corner)

[*V°*]

1st   *Joan Stop Soph I cant hold my hat*

2d   *Soph No I cant; hurry on quick*
         (runs into a wheel barrow)

3d   *(little girl) in great affright, "hey ma'am, you'l break the wheelbarrow!*

4th   *Gentleman in a roaring laughter—*
        "Are you much hurt Miss?"

> *This atrocious cold weather & slippery walking is very unpleasant in the streets. . . . We have had such odious weather that I've been out no where except to Peales—one day last week when Joan & I were going there, we thought we'd be blown away to the clouds—I never felt any thing like the wind, it blew our bonnets in our faces so we could not see, I ran foul of a wheelbarrow, nearly killed a little girl with terror, and a gentleman with laughing. . . .*
>
> [S to H, 5 December 1831]

[*V°*]

Up Market Street he turned
To take a last long look
Of the pictures and the pealing room
and the tin hung on a crook–
He listened to Peales' tones
So familiar to his ear–
And the Soldier on his elbow leant
And looked exceeding queer!

Mademoiselle, voici votre petite boite–

[*V°*]   *December 14ᵗʰ 1831. Wednesday.*

Charlotte came down from Philadᵃ with me. She had had a wooden box made for her hat which was large enough to have held herself. While the astonished driver was locating this genteel little bandbox over our heads, Mr. Ashhurst handed Lotte into the stage & then we drove off– After going about a dozen squares, the stage stopped–When several minutes had elapsed, one of the passengers inquired "Whats the matter?" "Why" said the driver "did I take in any one at yon place where I stopped?" "Well," said the poor driver "I know I got her box, but I didn't notice if I got her" We then understood he meant Charlotte & informed him she was in, just in time to prevent his turning back after her–off we went again, in a roar at the idea of Lotte's being so eclipsed by her baggage! we had a very pleasant journey, & no more adventures, except a fright lest Charlottes box should cause us to stick fast in the Brandywine bridge & the Wilmingtonians have to come & scratch us out, which catastrophe happily did not occur– [S to H, 22 December 1831]

That very week of December, Richard made his farewell visit to "the pealing room," the artist's studio in Market Street.

The same week brought a small contingent of Brandywine inhabs—Evelina, Brother Bidermann, and Papa—to Philadelphia. A sudden cold spell having frozen the river and closed navigation, Papa was forced to hire a carriage for the homeward journey of the entourage, which by then included Eleuthera, her portrait completed at last. Victorine in a letter to Eleuthera remarked what a pity it was that she, who wished to be in Philadelphia, should have had to return, while "poor Sophie who would be so much happier at home is obliged to stay–and then what is to become of Charlotte?" Sophie expressed her frustration to Henry:

> *You may think I am not a little provoked at being obliged to remain behind, when Charlotte & I are so anxious to get to the Brandywine together. However, it can't be helped, as Peale has not done with me, and tho' I cannot but be a little weary of the affair, the idea that we are doing it to please Papa, would make a far more disagreeable & tiresome situation pleasant.* [s to h, 5 December 1831]

For once, Sister Vic sounded a sympathetic note when she urged Sophie not to hurry Mr. Peale too much, or he

> *would not finish you as well as Eleuthera– when he painted us, he hurried Evelina's too much and the consequence was that her picture is very inferior to mine.* [v to s, December 1831]

As it turned out, there was no need for concern. Exactly three weeks and three days after Sophie's first sitting, Peale put the last stroke to her likeness, and by all accounts it was in fact superior to Eleuthera's. Whether it was the lively companionship of friends or the brisk walks up Market Street or simply her determination to maintain a cheerful demeanor, Sophie succeeded so well in disguising her natural shyness that Peale mistook her for the more outgoing of his two subjects. It was "lively, thoughtless Tata" who was painted with a sad and tearful countenance, whereas Sophie had glowing cheeks to match the rosebuds in her hand. Victorine was amused by the artist's reversal of their dispositions, but she was not amused by the fur tippet that Peale placed on Eleuthera's shoulders.

> *What possessed you to have such a thing put on, my dear? I thought we agreed that the more simple the dress was the better, and to be muffled up in a tippet is a strange notion.* [v to e, December 1831]

Nor was she pleased that Peale had taken only a three-quarter view of Sophie, which did not show "the whole of our sister's pretty face." The subject herself had mixed feelings when she was finally liberated:

I took my last sitting to Mr. Peale on Monday; & tired as I was of trotting up Market St, I could not help feeling regret at parting from the painting room, where, after all, I spent many pleasant hours. Mr. Peale is a very agreeable man, having travelled a good deal & his profession thrown him into the society of many eminent persons. He has painted me with two <u>rosebuds</u> in the <u>paw</u> that hangs over the sofa, tell Richard this. I was <u>shocked</u> at it, But I could not persuade him to omit them. [s to h, 22 December 1831]

No amount of determination to be unnoticed could quell the interest of the family and the curiosity of neighbors when the finished portraits arrived on the Brandywine early in March of 1832. Sophie's joy at being back in familiar surroundings was unmistakable.

Shores of the Tanco, March 3, 1832, Saturday morning,
In the parlour—Vic trotting in & out talking—
Eleu playing the <u>most bewitching</u> of waltzes in my ear. . . .

Dearest Hal, Last evening Meta & I returned from the other shores & found Vic, Tat, & Pol in conclave assembled, in our parlour. . . . Our pictures have all come home. Tell Richard that Papa's & mine are considered very good, Papa's is indeed excellent, I never saw a better one of anyone. Eleu & I are hung in our parlour, but Papa has given his to Alfred; we were sorry we could not keep it here, it is so delightful to have it to look at—But Papa wished it, & Alfred of course has a right to it & he is delighted as you may suppose—Eleu's looks as if she were going to cry—mine has too red hair, but all to that it is thought a good likeness—he has stuck a couple of dirty looking rosebuds in my hand, which I don't admire. Vic & Lina's pictures & Grandpapa's have been varnished & the whole concern framed anew & they look very well . . . Oh I must tell you a good one of the architect—Did not you & Dick go & see those chefs d'oeuvres de l'art, M^r & Mrs Boyds portraits, painted by that prince of itinerant daubers, yclept <u>West</u>, who sojourned some time on these shores? If not, you have heard them described I am sure—Well, the day we were hung, (I mean <u>in effigy</u>) The architect was the person who performed the deed—Voulant me faire un joli compliment, as he held my semblance in his clutches, he exclaimed, "Well indeed Miss Sophia, this here is so <u>natural</u>, I declare I dont *believe M*ʳ *West himself could have beat it!"–How we wanted to roar, as we thought of the rage Peal would be in, if he knew he had been compared to such a dauber–*

Despite her personal regard for Peale, Sophie could not resist impishly caricaturing the portraits done for Papa.

In the afternoon, Charles came over, & docteur Bridet, & with them C. Vandyke & Tinshanks to see our pictures–We were amused at Tinshanks qui voulait faire le Connaisseur–He heard some one say that Grandpapa's picture (which you know Peale himself painted when in France) was painted in France, & therefore he imagined it must have been painted by a French artist–so il s'extasieait before it, exclaiming, "regardez donc comme celui la est superieur! voyez cette chaire, c'est cela qui est naturel, qu'elle difference de cela et des autres! Voyez comme les couleurs sont naturels! c'est cela qui s'appelle peindre." &c &c while we were ready to roar, knowing they had all been painted by the same man–from which however, as from all the occurrences of life, a useful lesson may be gathered–viz, that whenever a person pretends to understand what he does not, he makes himself ridiculous– [S to H, 10 March 1832]

[V°]

–Do let me compare you with your portrait; my dear, will you permit me?

–Certainly, ma'am.

–Look a little aside. There–Do look serious my dear. Do look serious, my dear, a little more serious.

KNIGHTS AND COURTIERS

*D*own the pebbled allées of the garden, among the sylvan glades near Eleutherian Mills, and through the pages of family letters moved a gracious group of knights and courtiers worthy of the Age of Chivalry. Influenced in part by her admiration of Sir Walter Scott's works, in part by her own inclination to romanticism, and by a desire to ensure the privacy of her letters, Sophie ennobled inhabs, overcreekers, friends, and acquaintances as she described their exploits.

> *We could not help feeling a constant inclination to laugh at "the knights," who were in "high spirits" & ridiculous beyond measure–* [S to H, 15 July 1830]

Especially in writing of the young suitors who visited the three du Pont daughters, Sophie adopted a light, fantasy-cloaked tone in her correspondence with Henry, himself endowed with the sobriquet "Marquis de Furioso," in honor of his famous quick temper.

Reports to the Marquis on the salubrity of various family pets gradually shortened, to be replaced by reports, rumored or true, of sundry engagements, weddings, and elopements.

> *Frank's last letter announced to us his engagement with a young lady of Philad^a, whom I believe you have seen over the creek. . . . It is Miss Caroline Morris–They were engaged just before Frank sailed, But as the young lady's mother was so ill at the time that her daughter could not speak to her on the subject, the affair was considered as undecided, & was kept a secret. . . . As for the girl herself, We know her very slightly indeed; she is not pretty;– But since she is to be Frank's wife, we will of course try our best to love her for his sake. . . . our excellent cousin Frank has always been as dear as a brother to us, & nothing that so nearly concerns him can fail to deeply interest us–* [S to H, 18 June 1830]

In a lighter vein, when housemaid Mary Green eloped with stableman James Mullen, Sophie depicted "the verdant tribe" as "upset as a disturbed ant hill!"

Her letters to Henry were laden with accounts of various beaux of their mutual acquaintance and their careers and the status of Brandywine social pursuits:

> *By the Bye, I heard from my aunt over the creek there was to be a dinner at Ellerslie yesterday, in honor of Mr*

Evans Young coming of age–I expect one of the <u>convives</u> got there in rather a melancholy state. Ella & Caroline were coming home from Wilmn They noticed a gig driving very fast & trying to pass them–They however kept ahead for a good while, & Ella said to Caroline, "I'd laugh if they were thrown out in the mud"–One of them they had recognized as that Henry Warner we met at Youngs last summer–Suddenly the gig dashed by them, & out bounced Henry Warner into a mud puddle, while one of his pumps flew off in the road!–Of course, (as he was not hurt) Ella & Caroline took the liberty of laughing–He must have been in a pretty plight to present himself before the Lady Wilhelmina– [3 January 1831]

The Philadelphia scene and its festivities also figured in Sophie's exchanges with Henry:

Dr Goddard was my groomsman for the evening, I could not help laughing when I saw myself seated on one of those azure sofas you admire so much, with this <u>perfect monkey</u> in human form beside me, "What a charming place for a flirtation" said he, "come lets have one–" "<u>I never flirt</u>" said I, in a <u>manner</u> which <u>convinced him</u> I spoke the <u>sincere truth</u>–There was a great patagonian of a physician there, Hough, I think his name was, an awkward pile of human flesh bristled out with whiskers–helping me to ice cream in his <u>gigantic</u> style, he <u>managed</u> to bestow a portion on my silk dress! I was shocked, but couldnt help laughing–I expect I can get it out with magnesia–

[S to H, 3 November 1832]

Having grown up in a fairly large family, with brothers and their friends at hand, Sophie was comfortable with the men she knew. She was unimpressed by posturing and ridiculed those who, like Lieutenant Petitgru, demonstrated their self-importance. She was not above being a tease. When William Breck, a tall young man, appeared regularly week after week for Saturday chess games with Lady Bristlebrow, Sophie named him the "Saturday Evening Post," after the new literary magazine.

Being the object of teasing, however, Sophie enjoyed not at all. She was especially hurt when Tat accused her of flirting with Tom Smith.

I hope you are now <u>convinced</u> that your teasings about Lord George Fitzallan were a <u>vile aspersion</u> on us both–He is as I always said, faithful to <u>his old allegiance</u>, & your gentle heart Miss du P. has no cause for <u>jealousy</u>.

[S to E, n.d.]

1 Tat, pouring the contents of the pitcher on the candle

[*V°*]

Soph in utter astonishment– "Why my dear, what are you doing"

Eleu awaking– "Oh why! I thought I was lighting the candle!"

Lotte "ha ha ha Thats a good story! what oblivion

Eleu– "Oh no! I was only looking if there is any water here to water the flowers but I see there's none"

Soph in much surprize "Why, the pitcher is full!"–

Yesterday morning I was up to the elbows in paste, being in the midst of a portfolio I was making for Clem^a_ Smith, when the sound of sleigh bells struck my startled ear & at the same moment Lotte rushed up stairs & came bounding into the room, dragging off her morning dress & shrieking that the Gilpins were arriving!!! I sprang up, & scraping the paste off my fingers, flung my hair in order (or rather disorder), squeezed-to Lotta's hook & eyes, & we tripped down to the parlour, & entered, after composing our visages parlour-fashion at the door– When lo! who should be with Sarah, Mary, & William, but Liet^nt Petigru! And oh, such a youth! . . . such a conceited forward, chattering puppy as he appeared to us! why, he set us all in a roar as soon as the door closed after him! He went up to Tom (whom he had never seen before) & said "Do you reside permanently here sir?" "No I reside in Philad^a " "Ah–well sir, I am going up to Philad^a this winter & I shall see you there–"(!!!) "I shall be happy to see you, sir (responds Tom gravely) I reside at the Poor House!" "Ah! indeed" answers Petigru nothing daunted, "well, that is often the finest house in the city, at least judging from Wilmington."

[S to H, 6 January 1831]

Whenever possible she took precautions to ward off jibes from Vic and Tat. Just before she served as first bridesmaid at the New Castle wedding of her friend Mary Black in July of 1832, she confided to her diary,

> *John Couper is to be my groomsman. I'm very glad, as I know him, slightly, & I think I shall not feel either awe or embarrassment towards him. I should have preferred Gray; as he is engaged I could not have been teased about him, and besides we are old friends.*

To avoid being teased, Sophie sought to hide her true feelings, even when it made her appear indifferent or cold to others. Secretly she compared herself with her more outgoing sister:

> *Sometimes I wish I had Eleu's ready wit & repartee. But then, I know, that it is a dangerous gift—And when I feel how often, even she, unintentionally & unconsciously wounds my feelings with it I should rather not possess it—*
>
> [DIARY, 28 July 1832]

She was well aware that Tat longed to marry and was pained at finding herself single at the age of twenty-six. Claiming official status in the Society of Tabbies, Sophie recorded,

> *My desire is, that my sister Eleu should marry & I remain single, to live with Pa & sister and to be their comfort & take care of them when they will grow old—* [DIARY, 5 February 1832]

To preserve that tabby status, Sophie shied away from romantic situations. The Reverend Mr. Pardee, walking to church with her along the Brandywine in May 1832, inquired whether she "was not *very* romantic" and tried to persuade her that being so was a harmless accompaniment to the fine scenery. He fared no better than John Goddard, and she reported the incident to Tat:

> *I must say I did not admire such conversation in a clergyman, particularly on his way to the pulpit—altogether his sermon & himself I did not like.*

For some two years, Sophie was courted by John Phillips of Philadelphia and Lenni. Of his first visit to the Brandywine, she wrote Henry:

> *Yesterday Ferdinand came over from Lenni, with a Mr Philips, their neighbour, whom I think I have mentioned to you before now—He is a very kind neighbour to the Lammots, who like him much—He appears to be an agre-*

able man, but his manners are so forward, that I was not pleased with him–I had never seen him till yesterday, yet he was as familiar with me as tho' I'd known him a long time–a thing which I neither admire, nor like, in a gentleman– [22 March 1830]

A young man of about thirty, with unusually large feet, Phillips sought to impress the du Pont sisters with his exceptional range of knowledge, exotic bouquets, thoughtful mementos, and interesting books and prints. On his many visits, all unannounced, he importuned the three sisters; he would even arrive in the morning before Vic's birds were fed. He discoursed on phrenology, botany, fireworks, and astronomy, among other topics. Vic, at least, was impressed, and fleetingly it seemed that the "Knight of Rockdale" might be courting *her*.

Vic said some half dozen times in the course of the evening– "How entertaining Phillips is" "he is really a very amusing man" &c, & at supper she actually–will you believe it?–actually poured out the tea into the sugar bowl! Oh how Mary & I did roar! [S to E, 27 October 1830]

Poor Phillips, who became known as Val de Peñas as well as the Knight of Rockdale, was unappreciated by Sophie except as a subject for caricature:

We had the pleasure of Phillips to supper sunday night, & I've had the headache ever since–car entre nous, I don't like him and he tires us to death sometimes though on the whole he is a well informed intelligent man. he is a great oddity–I take the liberty of laughing at him & carricaturing him– [S to H, 22 February 1831]

Sophie recited candidly in her letters the many subjects on which the Knight soliloquized, as well as the poorly disguised methods she devised for escaping his company. When she visited the R. Smiths in Philadelphia or in Lenni, she also avoided the company of his family, the "Phillipians," for they wished to entertain her and develop the social connection. In November 1830, she did attend a ball at the Phillips's home in Philadelphia in the company of Mrs. Smith, Caroline Morris, and Elenora Lammot:

We went at 9 oclock & returned a little before one–I was very much amused–I had never been to a large dance–and it was some years since I had at all mingled in society–every thing therefore was a novelty to me. The ladies dresses particularly afforded me an ample field of entertainment–They dress their hair now about two feet high orna-

mented with flowers or feathers or ribbons or all three. . . . Mr. John Phillips was there of course. . . . He is very tall & very awkward, I had to dance with him, Imagine the tongs a little bent, shuffling about the floor with a small andiron, & you'll have the scene exactly– [S to H, 1 December 1830]

Lady Bristle Brow

By the bye, we call her nothing but Lady Bristlebrow here, and I will tell you why–You know Lewis Rumford pretended to tell her fortune. She, thinking I knew nothing of it, came and repeated it to me; "and only think!" she said "he is to have bristly red eyebrows! only think how horrid! bristly eye brows!" and every one she has seen since, with very ugly eyebrows she exclaims "Ah! that must be the one Lewis meant! see how hideous he is!" So that we call her lady Bristle brow, from that. [S to H, 24 June 1828]

Chapter Extracted from a new unpublished & unfinished novel by an American little Unknown

An old rusty gig and two saddle Horses were fastened at the door of that smoke-blackened brick building well known to the inhabitants of Delaware County as the Marcus Hook tavern. . . .

It was however easy to discern that he of the woollen stocking wished to shorten the interview and was impatient to pursue his journey. . . . he took a hasty leave of his acquaintances and humming melodiously . . . he advanced to mount his courser. — Whether the anticipated delight which caused his tender heart to throb, bewildered his optical faculties, or whether his mind had outrun his body to the presence of his "ladye love" it is not for us to determine — but . . . he was interrupted by a start from his horse whose nose had suddenly come in contact with his master's whip and who (more attentive to the gesture than the music) broke his bridle and scampered away kicking up his heels through the thin mud and melting snow. . . .

Meanwhile our unlucky hero impeded by his accoutrement had to use his utmost exertions to wade through the mud. Not unlike the famous knight Rinaldo di Mont'Albano when armed cap a pie he pursued his charger flying through woods and thickets. . . . Wildfire (the knight of the woollen stocking's palfrey) guided rather by his own than by his master's wishes after cutting a few capers and splashing his pursuer from head to foot, ran to the well remembered stable, where he had been sometimes fed in cases of emergency. [1831]

Mr Cicero Crumb performing the exploit which quite won the heart of a certain lady—

Friday 26th August Mrs R. S. Smith returned from Tusculum escorted by Mr Alexander Reid. They paid a long morning visit, and invited us all to go over sociably very soon—Mr Reid observing that his sister had dropped a piece of gingerbread on the mat started forward & gracefully picked it up: which act of nicety & economy greatly delighted the manufacturer of said gingerbread—

["The Tancopanican Chronicle," 1831]

La belle assemblee

I have a laughable story of a partner of hers at the Phillips ball. . . . In the midst of the dance, he exclaims, "excuse me ma'am" & darts off, leaving Ella petrified, not knowing what to do, & the whole set put out till John Phillips rushed forward & took his place—He reappeared at the end of the set but made no apoly to Ella & avoided her all the rest of the evening. Every one pronounced him the rudest of bears—Now the explanation of the whole matter "has come to light." . . . It appears, in the first efforts to dance, his suspenders gave way entirely and he was obliged to hold up his pantaloons, the descent of which you will allow, would have been distressing—(for himself & spectators) His excuse to Ella was necessarily abrupt & he hurried to the door, which being much crowded at that moment, his further retreat was impeded—In this dilemma he felt some one pulling his suspenders, which had found their way down, & turning round he beheld little Caroline Phillips, who exclaimed aloud, "What is this!" [S to H, 10 December 1830]

I happened to cast my eyes thro' the pantry window, & beheld Phillips–his gigantic form enveloped in a huge great coat, his immeasurable feet circumscribed by a curious piece of mechanism he denominated overshoes. . . . & his round caput decorated by a little "seal skin bonnet, old & grim"–In this bewitching array he entered the house, was ushered by the gigling sir Sprol into the dining room (we having no fire in the parlour) & Pol & I had to seat ourselves & endure his presence for two long hours–Uncoiling himself beside the grate he raised his ponderous pedes to the genial fender–I thought more than once of those lines you & Octavius used to quote, "His feet were small & delicately shaped, For full ten miles the ground they scraped–" After he had been here about half an hour, Sprol enters "Why sir, your Bucephale is freezing there at the gate this half hour"– "Well" he says "Have him put back in the stable, for I've found such comfortable quarters" (pointing to the grate) "that he may wait"–Oh with what dismay Pol & I heard this! the birds were not fed, at last I fed them before him, hoping he'd take the hint–but no, he waited till he was completely toasted, & had t[reated] us to learned discourses on botany, craniology, embroidery, anatomy, [word missing], drawing, poetry &c &c &c &c– [S to H, 25 December 1830]

[*V°*]

A travelling costume
Sunday Jany 23^d 1831–
que je suis beau!

We had just got the room into grand disorder & kicked up all the car-
pets, when Mary looking out of the window cries, "There's Phillips!"–
"No–no!–no!" we shrieked for we thought him safely snowed up at
rock-dale–(his place) we flew to the window & behold 'twas he! in the
most complete travelling equipage, so that only his eye was visible, he
looked like a Cyclops– [S to H, 27 January 1831]

Ursa Major   Ursa Minor

Vic says she leaves it to me to describe the exhibition of betes
curieuses–My dear, I was fated to see the said creatures, & am
glad now I did see them as they were worth it–We met one animal
there whom we had not expected to see, I mean Ursa Minor! with
his lady mother & Mr & Mrs J. Warner–He flew up to Ella (who
accompanied us) the moment we entered–He was very tame &
civil–Quite an appropriate place for an encounter with the bear,
was it not? [S to E, October 1830]

There was no question of acceptance when Papa transmitted to his youngest daughter the Knight's proposal of marriage:

Papa with gt delicacy said "Mr P. I thought best after what you told me this morning to go see my daughter, She bade me say that she was grateful for the proof of esteem you have given her but that she cannot return the sentiments of attachment you have for her—Papa paused—He [Phillips] gave a grunt—dead pause ensued— "Mr Phillips said Papa I hope that this will not make any difference in our friendship"—not a word did he say—When Papa saw this he took up a newspaper and read a few minutes then addressed the knight on the subject of the tarriff on which they talked as if nothing had occurred. [E to V, 29 January 1832]

Then, after listing other bulletins from Eleutherian Mills, Eleu added, "In all this affair what shocks Sophy most is the *grunt.*"

Sophie's sentiments of attachment had in fact for some time been directed closer to home. She was deeply in love with her cousin Frank, who was due to return from a three-year tour of duty in the Mediterranean.

Frank has arrived! He is safe, he is once more in his native land In a few weeks perhaps in <u>one</u> we shall see him. . . . When I think of seeing him again amongst us, all seems delightful but immediately I think of his marriage—Oh that <u>thought</u> is still too painful! [DIARY, 6 May 1832]

Frank's betrothal to Caroline Morris had been distressing to Sophie from the instant she heard of it. Her feelings became so evident to her sisters that they suggested she had personal motives in opposing the prospective marriage. But she admitted only to the fear that Frank would not be loved as he deserved. True, she had indulged in hero worship since her cousin had joined the Navy soon after the War of 1812. All the younger du Ponts shared her awe of Cousin Frank, and any news of his accomplishments was quickly passed along in the family. Only in her diary did Sophie reveal the constancy and intensity of her feelings toward her "primo hermano," as she called him.

I feel that sort of desolate, lonely feeling, as if my <u>heart</u> were alone on earth & vainly yearned for companionship with some that could feel as I do. On Friday I heard Frank had arrived the night before & would be over to see me; Till he came, I was so agitated I could scarce do any thing—was this right? I know it was <u>not</u>, for it was not with

joyful feelings: & I thought more on the painful results his return might have, than on the great blessing & joy we
should feel his safe return to be—I was calm when he was here, & cold too, I fear—But as soon as he was gone, the
tears would come—I sat down & let them flow for some moments, I scarce knew why— [DIARY, 29 May 1832]

There was no need for tears. Several weeks later, in the summer of 1832, Frank ended his engagement.

In later years Frank confided that he had first felt drawn to Sophie when he returned from his cruise on the
North Carolina in 1827, to find his merry little cousin transformed into a modest, animated, and intelligent young
woman. When she appeared indifferent to his overtures, he was not immediately discouraged, but judged that
ever-present family might be the reason. Therefore, hoping to press his suit, he arranged to be in Philadelphia
while she was there visiting the Lammots. Caught in a whirl of parties and teas, Sophie responded to Cousin
Frank's daily visits with seeming indifference. He was thus vulnerable to his mother's urging that he direct his
attentions to Caroline, the wealthy Philadelphia belle to whom he impulsively became engaged prior to his
departure on the Mediterranean cruise of the _Ontario_.

To fellow officer Garrett Pendergrast, Frank confessed that he soon realized the betrothal represented a
grave mistake in judgment on his part, for their correspondence proved how incompatible he and Caroline
really were. During the entire term of his sea duty on the _Ontario_ he worried over finding some honorable
means of extricating himself from what promised to be an inharmonious union. In Sardis, while seated amid the
ruins of an ancient church, he discovered that he had unconsciously carved the name Sophie into an overturned
stone column.

After the termination of his engagement, Sophie's letters recounted almost daily visits from Frank and the
gift of a specimen of lava, her "talisman," from him on her birthday in September. By October, when she and
Frank and Alfred and Meta were chosen to represent the du Ponts at Mary Lammot's wedding to Thomas
Hounsfield, family friends began to remark Sophie's growing attachment to her cousin. Sophie's description of
the wedding at Lenni centered on the bridesmaids' activities:

The whole wedding party staid at Lenni that night—and as we young girls, ten of us slept in one room, you may
think there was little rest that night, & plenty of laughing & talking— [S to H, 8 November 1832]

It was February before Sophie herself "dared to dream of earthly felicity." After an excursion with Frank to New Castle, she wrote to Henry:

It was not until our ride home that I had the least idea that our cousin's regard for me was <u>more</u> than that of <u>a</u> <u>cousin</u>. [4 March 1833]

Brimming with happiness, she wrote Tat at the same time:

I am more convinced than ever that Love is a species of insanity—I can now confess that I speak from experience, since I tell you that during a fit of <u>mental aberration</u> I have been persuaded to renounce the society of <u>Tabbies</u>—what you'll think of my defection I know not—But you must lay all the blame on Cousin Frank, as the mischief was all owing to him. I am very glad you were away, for I could never have stood all your <u>reproaches</u> on the subject.

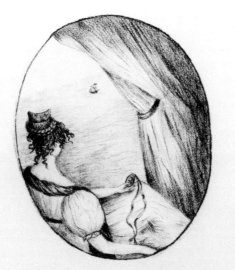

The sea-breeze waves her silken hair—
She doth not feel the ocean air
    Tho' chill its breath may be.
She only feels that freshening gale
Is wafting for her lover's sail
    Across the silent sea—

[*V°*]　*Preparations for a wedding—adorning the paranymphe—*

Eleu (in a voice of distress)　O Sarah!　Charlotte!　Oh relieve

me!

Oh Ill discompose the altitude of my puffs!—

The fifth anniversary of our marriage. . . . This day has been as cool, as bright, almost as cloudless as that in 1833, in which my eyes wakened so reluctantly. When I left my place by dear Lotte's side, which I was to occupy <u>no more</u>, what sadness we felt; while she breathed her fears that new ties should weaken that which bound me to her, and received the oft repeated assurance no other love could ever interfere with the sacred bond between our hearts—The morning of that day was passed in seeing many of my young friends, receiving presents, many, & beautifully, & kindly given— [DIARY, 27 June 1838]

With considerable elation Frank announced the engagement to his family and close friends. "A woman of sound sense & education, but an angel of purity & of sensibility" was his description of Sophie in a letter of March 4, 1833, to Naval Surgeon John S. Wily. Adding "She is pretty too!," Frank confided,

What I had told you of my suspicions as to her feelings were but too true—I was the only man that had ever excited the soft feeling, & so humble (which is her only fault) is her opinion of herself that she had persuaded herself that I never could think of her—

The betrothal met with the complete approbation of the entire family. Frank's mother felt herself "renovated" by the news, while Papa embraced Frank and told him he "had long wished it." Victorine was ecstatic, and she quickly steered the household into preparations for the wedding. Depicting himself and Sophie as the "enfants gâtés" of the two du Pont families, Frank reported that "every body had laid out the match, & each & every one was anxious to claim it as the offspring of his own imagination."

Sophie spent the next three months absorbed in the "ennuious" tasks of arranging her trousseau and making the prescribed visits to friends in the Wilmington, Philadelphia, and Washington areas. Frank fretted through the inevitable problems of choosing attendants and setting the earliest possible wedding date, which depended on Henry's arrival home after his graduation from West Point. Then on June 27, 1833, after spending a sunny day with her dearest friends and loved ones—a day that included the drawing of a caricature by the bride as she watched Eleuthera being dressed as bridesmaid for the ceremony—Sophie married her Frank in the parlor at Eleutherian Mills.

THE SPRINGS: AN EPILOGUE

*F*estivities honoring the bride and groom lasted a month, until they left on a short wedding trip north to "the chosen residence of Eolus" (West Point) and Trenton Falls. From the canal boat on which they traveled, Sophie wrote Meta on August 24 about one stop they made:

> *Frank came in to tell me he had found a beautiful street he wished me to see, before it was too dark—I jumped up instantly & seizing my bonnet, we sallied forth & took a delightful walk, half by moonlight, thro' one of the prettiest streets imaginable—Some of the houses were literally <u>covered</u> with creepers, & had little gardens filled with flowers: two of them had large apricot trees <u>trelised</u> against their walls, and loaded with fruits—I was much pleased with all I saw of Utica, & think it the prettiest little town I've seen.*

Caricatures had no part during this trip, or during the years that followed. Sophie did not regard sketching as appropriate to the life of a proper matron. The duties of hearth and home, the duties of religion and correspondence, and even reading—all took precedence over the frivolity of drawing. Sophie continued to keep her journal, but she stopped reaching for her sketchbook after she crossed the creek to live at Louviers.

Becoming an overcreeker was wrenching for Sophie, so strong were her ties to home. But she was warmly welcomed to Frank's home by his mother, his sisters, Amelia and Julia, Julia's three young children, and Cousin Ella—all family members she knew and loved. There, too, French was the language of the house. In only two respects was Louviers alien to Sophie's previous environment: her cousins did not share her taste in reading but preferred lighter fare, and all the women of the household were devoutly Roman Catholic. Sophie's Protestant evangelistic enthusiasm tended to be divisive, especially in Frank's absence on active duty in the Navy.

During the early years of their marriage, Frank's active duty was deferred because of Sophie's health. Besides a recurrence of her knee problem, she had a serious back ailment and a bursitis-like complaint that forced her to write with her left hand much of the time. In accordance with the medical practice of the day she was confined to her bedroom, a parlor sofa, or a sedan chair used to transport her to the garden. Trips across the creek to see her sisters were a rarity, and periods of intellectual isolation became an inevitable part of her married life. With her husband by her side, she had a valued reading companion; their discussions provided

Warm Springs. . . . The most abundant of these gushes from the earth in the middle of a large octagonal basin of mason work covered with a wooden building having an opening at the top, & four neat & comfortable rooms on as many sides for the accommodation of bathing. This bath is thirty eight feet in diameter; & the temperature of water 96 degrees—It is one of the most curious & beautiful objects I have seen, the water is pure & translucent to an almost dazzling degree, & rises in ceaseless flow, accompanied by showers of bright gleaming air bubbles—

[S to Clementina Smith, 21 July 1837]

significant intellectual stimulation and helped cement their lasting relationship. Frank fully encouraged Sophie's knowledge of his naval aspirations, the politics of the service, national and international events, and the many places he visited around the world. He sought her opinions and often paid her the compliment of following her advice. In time they came, too, to share religious views. Their correspondence during their more than thirty years of married life reveals deep affection. On her fifth anniversary Sophie wrote:

I thank God, that each succeeding year has made us greet this day with more pleasure—with more heartfelt joy & thankfulness for the blessing we possess in each other's affection! How comparatively light are all the ills of the world, when we can share them together in the full communion of true & loving hearts! Surely that must be the right kind of love, which grows deeper & fonder every year! [DIARY, 27 June 1838]

But when Frank was ordered to sea, Sophie, who had previously cherished solitude, had to cope with loneliness. Her diaries record, first, her nostalgia for past happiness, then her search for life's meaning, her struggle to accept life on its own terms, and, finally, a kind of pervasive melancholy. Year upon year passed with medical consultations, an unending quest for relief from pain by trips to healing waters, both springs and seashore, and a period of addiction to that Valium of the nineteenth century, morphine.

In 1837, Dr. Horner of Philadelphia recommended a trip to the Virginia springs, and Frank at once set about making the necessarily complicated arrangements. Sophie's friend Eliza Schlatter, who was suffering from an eye ailment, accompanied the pair on their journey south. In her vacation baggage, Sophie packed her drawing equipment, in case there might be subjects of interest on this trip designed for healthful recreation. And so among her last sketches is a series depicting Warm Springs. Drawn for the most part realistically, they present traces of the merriment of former years. With a twinkle in her eye, Sophie includes the only known carics of her Frank.

We rode about three miles an hour, over roads that required all the care & skill of our intelligent driver to pass without incessant jolting— Tho' on the whole they were far better than travellers generally find them, There not having been much heavy rain.

[S to Clementina Smith, 21 July 1837]

*Sometimes suddenly turning round a lofty group of almost perpendicular rocks with wild flowers, & vines, & shrubs,
trailing down from their crevices—while within perhaps a foot of the carriage wheel, the road abruptly overlooked a
precipice, gazing down into whose far abyss inspired feelings of height & sublimity I cannot describe—*

[S to Clementina Smith, 21 July 1837]

We left Fredericksburg on the morning of the 4ᵗʰ of July & were eight days in reaching this place, the first day we travelled thirty miles, but never accomplished so much in the same time afterward. . . . The whole country we traversed was fresh, luxuriant & beautiful beyond description. . . . It was just the kind of country to delight <u>me</u>, covered chiefly with woods, wild & picturesque. . . . Anon, emerging suddenly, we beheld the open fields with their pale green crops of oats, or golden wheat, and the log farmhouses on the slope while the partridges whistled over our heads, & the shining faced little negroes ran out to see us pass. But the crossing of the mountains themselves was the most enchanting part of the whole to me. . . . the eye could range over a vast expanse of country, valley, & wood, & mountain rising after mountain, till the last blue summits mingled with the sky— <u>You know</u> how passionately I have loved those wilder features of creation, where we more immediately trace the impress of the great Author's hand—& you may faintly imagine their effect upon me, after four years almost constant confinement to a chamber of sickness. . . . The settlement of the springs, consisting of two large brick hotels with long piazzas in front, & several rows of brick or log cabins, has nothing very pretty about it, except its situation, in an undulating valley completely embosomed in the mountains. Altho' there is so little company here that we had our choice of rooms anywhere, we preferred a cabin, to be nearer the spring; & we could not have made a better choice. . . . How I wish you were here this calm afternoon, to behold with me the declining sunshine filling the woody sides of these towering mountains, while shade is gradually stealing over the verdant fields on the lower slopes—the deep blue sky above, the fresh air shivering in the acacia's foliage, & the birds calling to one another from trees & groves—There is an air of <u>primeval peace</u> pervading this sweet valley, that makes me think of Miltons descriptions of the first eras of creation, & of the days too, when the foot of the red men alone pressed this sod—& surely in these "high places" they must have come to worship "the Great Spirit.". . . We expect to leave here Monday for the hot springs five miles distant. We have not decided whether we will make any stay there, or only remain a day—Afterward we are to go to the <u>White Sulphur</u>, the repair of fashion, where there are already 250 human beings congregated; I suppose we will not stay there long, as from the trial of drinking sulphureous water we made here, I doubt any of them will agree with us—afterward Dʳ Horner prescribes our going to the Sweet Springs which are chalybeate, with delightful cold baths. . . .

[S to Clementina Smith, 21 July 1837]

About three weeks later, in a letter in French to Sir Sprol, Sophie described their progress through the next springs. At Hot Springs there were but some seventy people, mostly cripples, but very gay. Then at White Sulphur, they found some five hundred fashionables. She explained to Sir Sprol that such crowds affected the availability of food. There was not the abundance of venison, chicken, vegetables, milk, and cream that they had encountered on their other stops, but the bread was good and the mutton not too hard. A shortage of chairs forced morning and afternoon visitors to improvise seating by using beds and trunks. At every meal during the evening an excellent group of musicians played, chiefly Italian music, but at the nightly balls most people went to watch, not to dance. Above all, Sophie was impressed by the cabins, tiny two-room houses, sometimes with a piazza; they strongly contrasted with the immense hotels in the north, which she described as full of "petites cellules où l'on étouffe les gens!"

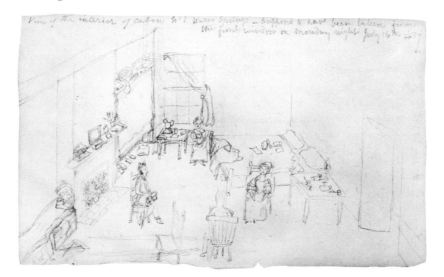

View of the interior of cabin N° 1 Warm Springs—Supposed to have been taken from the front window on Monday night June 16th 1837

Our domicile consists of two rooms communicating, in which we have every thing we want to make us comfortable, & a very attentive & obliging maid to bring us our meals & all we wish for— The front door (from my room) opens towards the roads, & on a path which leads up to the hotel! The door of Elizas room leads out into a green sloping meadow, planted with trees, in the centre of which are the warm springs. [S to Clementina Smith, 21 July 1837]

Being <u>toted</u> to the bath-

They were making hay in the undulating meadow, which added to the picturesque effect of the scenery There is here a very convenient <u>chaise a porteur</u> in which I am carried, or the <u>blackies</u> here express it, <u>toted</u>, from one place to another– [S to Clementina Smith, 21 July 1837]

This afternoon I was again interrupted by Elisa & Frank coming for me, to take me down into the <u>second</u> meadow to see the place where a rivulet of cold water meets & joins a stream of warm that flows from the springs– The waters flow awhile together without mingling, distinguishable to the eye by the superior clearness & brilliancy of the warm stream; you can put your hand into the two currents so that half yr fingers are immersed in cold, & half in warm water at the same time– [S to Clementina Smith, 21 July 1837]

Spout bath at the Warm Springs—

There are several other springs of the same kind in the meadow—round one a platform is built with benches, under shady trees, for those who drink the water, which notwithstanding its odour of half spoiled eggs & its warmth, is not very nauseous to the taste—Another bath house contains four small baths, into one of which a spout is arranged for the benefit of those who are recommended to take douches. I have tried this at Dr Horner's request & think it of service to me, as well as the bathing. [S to Clementina Smith, 21 July 1837]

This was her only trip to the springs. In other years she and Frank vacationed for several weeks in August at Cape May, where they enjoyed ocean bathing. Despite her delicate health, Sophie did travel occasionally with her husband—to Norfolk, Boston, Alexandria, Washington, D.C., and New York, as well as to Philadelphia. Their only extensive absence from home together was occasioned by Frank's appointment as Superintendent of the 1853 New York Exhibition of the Industry of All Nations, better known as the Crystal Palace, after its successful British predecessor. With some misgivings he stepped into the highly controversial job, which entailed an unrealistic deadline, a quarreling board, a dubious financial outlook, and a leaky roof. And he wanted Sophie at his side.

The pair left Louviers in the first bloom of spring to spend the next few months in rooms they rented at 7 Waverly Place in New York. Of the whole experience Sophie wrote:

> *The Crystal Palace I enjoyed without alloy, as a child enjoys its pleasure. Everything there interested my mind and charmed my eye. Shut for twenty years, almost wholly in the house & in the country, I had scarcely ever entered a common store, so that a thousand things were new & interesting to me that could not be so to others. The society & conversation of some intelligent minds, too, was an enjoyment I especially appreciated. . . . I read a great deal, too, in New York—a thing I never can do at home. But what was the chief source of my happiness there & the <u>one</u> thing that enabled me to enjoy all the others & to be benefitted by them, was not being parted from my husband.*

> [DIARY, 25 September 1853]

Sophie cherished mementos of their successful stay in the city. A friend rescued for her William Cullen Bryant's first draft of the ode he wrote to be sung at the grand opening of the exposition; the Committee presented Frank with a handsome silver service in appreciation of his endeavors; Frank persuaded her to make some purchases. Other souvenirs were less tangible: lectures from Herbert Minton on the subject of porcelain; new friendships with the Maurys and the Syleses, who would play a future role in Frank's experiences in China and Sophie's own support of foreign missions; renewed contact with the Cazenove family members living near New York. In retrospect Sophie fondly described her last visit to the Crystal Palace, "a fairy scene of enchantment, the beautiful building lighted with thousands of shining stars."

Cape May, 1839

In the years that followed she rarely ventured farther from home than Philadelphia. Widowed in 1865, Sophie devoted the last twenty-three years of her life to work with her husband's papers, to the support of missions of the Episcopal church, and to promoting the unity of the younger generation of du Ponts, many of whom were living far from her beloved Brandywine valley. Of Papa's children, only Henry survived her. Only Henry could review those vivid scenes of youth—the boisterous escapades of the Lavatory Company, the young women of the Brandywine marching to Fortress Monroe, and making war on the wasps to the tune of the "Marseillaise"—as he thought back beyond his West Point days to the world of Sophie's carics.

Presented to me by her excellencissimo
highness Miss G P D C April 1826

horned poppy
alias horrid

NATURAL HISTORY

From early childhood, Sophie had full access to the natural history books in the family library. Young as she was, she could catch the enthusiasm of Bon Papa's stories about his French colleagues Buffon, Cuvier, and Michaux. Exercising great care, she was permitted to admire the tiny, tinted illustrations in the family set of Buffon's volumes describing the earth's animals, birds, and fish. She sensed her father's delight when Michaux sent him a copy of his work on American trees. And she could remember years later the stories told in the family about the visit of the eccentric naturalist Rafinesque to the Brandywine.

Sophie was encouraged to observe and appreciate nature. On those rare afternoons when Papa was home and had finished work for the day, he and Mama took the children to walk by the riverbank—identifying and talking about the plants, rocks, and trees as they went. The first of May was one of the most exciting days of the year, when family tradition decreed a search for the flowers of spring, and all the inhabs took part in the expedition.

Romping with Henry through the woods and meadows by Eleutherian Mills, Sophie had ample opportunity to exercise the sharp powers of observation developed through those happy years. After their morning lessons they roamed the untamed environs, free to follow the small streams that tumbled over the rocks into the Brandywine—Squirrel Run, Crayfish Run, Dauphin's Run, Pancake Run. They explored the steeply wooded banks, where they discovered caves and secret crevices among huge boulders and a great variety of specimens of insects and minerals.

> *Forgetting time and change, I can almost fancy myself the wild little romp that built mud forts, & dams, and <u>moss gardens</u> with you—when you were my only companion and <u>you yourself</u> had no playmate, no friend you preferred to your sister! They <u>were happy days, dearest Harry</u>. . . . [S to H, 22 March 1830]*

Encouraged by Alfred to start their own cabinet of curiosities, Sophie and Henry collected almost instinctively. Henry followed his brother's example as a collector of rocks and minerals. In the spring of 1822 Sophie made a catalogue of more than a hundred minerals in their collection. But her enthusiasm was for insects. That same year, on her birthday, she presided at the first official meeting of the Entomological Society of the Brandywine. Its new president, known to her fellow members as Lady Locusta Longhorns, recorded the names and learned appellations of the other officers: Lady

Anchora Strawberrys (Eleuthera), secretary; Lady Ephemera Grasshopper (Polly Simmons), reader; Sir Fire-Coloured Tweezer (Henry), perforator; Sir Light Bug (Alfred), turpentiner. Their collections increased steadily, but the Society only occasionally—when honorary membership was bestowed on a favored visitor. (Anne Callender Lewis was elected under the title of Czarina of the Cockroaches.) In the serious pursuit of entomological expertise, Sophie indulged her interest in scientific experimentation and made early use of her artistic talents as well. Recording her efforts to determine if insects have an auxiliary sight ability, Lady Locusta reported:

> On the head of some insects between their two eyes, there are three little shining dots, through which it is said they see as well as through their eyes. I wished to ascertain the truth of this and for that purpose I took a locust and covered his eyes with thick gum, but the locust appeared perfectly blind. When it flew it hit itself against every thing it met. —I then took some clear water and washed off the gum, when the locust regained his sight and flew away on a tree. [S to H, 22 July 1825]

Among the papers of the Entomological Society are minute drawings of a caterpillar's movement across a flat surface, along with a group of sketches from nature to "exemplify the seven classes of insects."

Within a month of its founding the Society lost the services of its official Perforator when Henry went away to school, in the fall of 1822. Formal "Memoirs" of the Society continued to be submitted, however, and meetings were held when vacations permitted. After neighbor Mary Gilpin went to school in England in 1823, she and Sophie maintained an informal sort of butterfly "exchange." And in the best Society tradition, the youngest du Pont of his generation, Lil, successfully raised a crop of silkworms in 1827, before the fad was widespread in America. In her letters to Henry, Sophie chronicled the minutiae of the Brandywine: a new "Big Chestnut" in the butterfly collection; samples of mica found in the quarry at the Way farm across the creek; Indian artifacts of serpentine found when the millrace was drained; a mushroom of unusual hue from the nearby woods.

Like sister Tat, Sophie executed delicate watercolors of many of the wildflowers that grew in profusion near Eleutherian Mills. Specimens of windflowers, hepaticas, violets, and *Lobelia Cardinalis* were dug up and replanted in parterres of the garden near the house. Both girls preferred the scientific names of the plants to their popular ones. And they often patterned their drawings after those in scientific publications of the day. They had been taught the value of copying accurately and considered it a valid drawing exercise, but with so many flowers at hand they most often drew from nature. Sophie, who especially enjoyed launching lengthy and demanding projects, did undertake to copy the bird prints of Wilson's *Ornithology*, but she did not progress very far toward her goal.

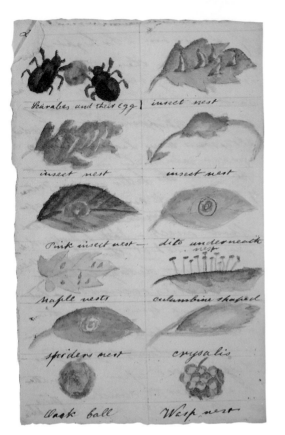

This insect I observed on a large yellow mushroom— Having but one specimen I was unable to become acquainted with its manners &c When alarmed it would leap to a considerable distance, like a flea &c— It is evidently of the order Aptera, being perfectly devoid of wings— Its legs are six in number — Antenna two, thick and transparent. As far as I can judge, I believe its food to consist solely of mushrooms—

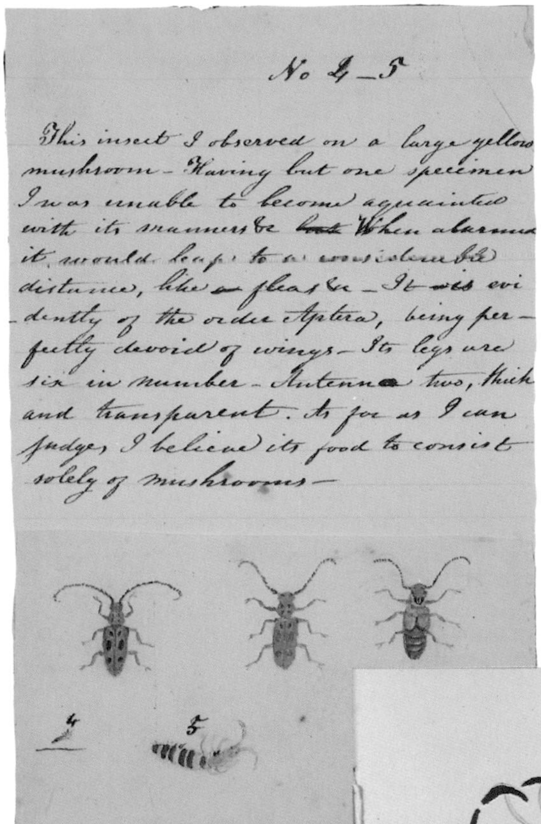

No 4 – 5

This insect I observed on a large yellow
mushroom – Having but one specimen
I was unable to become acquainted
with its manners &c ~~but~~ When alarmed
it would leap to a considerable
distance, like a flea &c – It ~~is~~ evi
-dently of the order Aptera, being per –
fectly devoid of wings – Its legs are
six in number – Antennæ two, thick
and transparent. As far as I can
judge, I believe its food to consist
solely of mushrooms –

4   5

Lepidoptera

Locusta Binghoon
President of
Entymological
Society 1823

Beyond the immediate family circle, Sophie's ever-growing knowledge of the natural world around her gained a degree of recognition. In 1832, Mary Gilpin proposed that Sophie

> *assist her in writing a work like the journal of a Naturalist about this country—Her plan was we should each keep a journal, &*
> *read, & obtain scientific information, & afterwards condense our observations . . . & informations, into a work like the above*
> *cited—She hinted that if we found it worthy afterwards, we might anonymously publish it! Oh dear! I was shocked at the bare*
> *idea of any word of <u>mine</u> in any way appearing in print! We talked the plan over all the way—My first impulse was to get off*
> *from the whole affair, because I've really not time to devote to it. . . . However I found her heart so fixed on it, & that she*
> *would be hurt if I positively declined all participation, because she seemed to think my disposition to do so arose from contempt*
> *at the idea, that I agreed to assist her with what little I could, if <u>she</u> undertook the work—But on condition of a positive promise*
> *that she would never mention me to any one as implicated in it. . . . The more I see of her, while I admire her <u>mind</u>, &*
> *education, & acquirements, the more I feel the impossibility of <u>loving</u> her as an intimate friend.* [DIARY, 28 November 1832]

There is no indication that such a work was ever actually begun.

However, Sophie's interest in natural history did continue throughout her life. She treasured the herbarium she painstakingly assembled; she delighted in the rock samples and shells that Frank brought home from his travels; she devoured travelogues that described the natural features of the farthest reaches of little-explored continents. While taking great pleasure in her knowledge of the scientific order of nature, she above all recognized in the world around her the full wonders of creation.

Artist unknown. *Young Ladies Sketching.* c. 1822. Pencil, 3⅝ x 6¼″.

LANDSCAPES

*D*uring her brief school attendance in Philadelphia, Sophie's course of study included drawing lessons with French artist-naturalist Charles Alexandre Lesueur, who had instructed Tat several years before and had accepted invitations to visit at Eleutherian Mills during the summer. While on the Brandywine he led some merry sketching sessions, in which Sophie participated even before her studies began. During these summertime expeditions, the formal classroom procedures of drawing from models in a prearranged sequence were left behind, and the company drew from nature. The enjoyment of his tutelage persisted after he returned to France, in the autumn of 1825, and in the years that followed the young du Pont ladies took sketch pads and crayons in hand to keep the Lesueur tradition alive. At Aunt Victor's request, Cousin Ella joined Sophie each Monday and Friday to sketch on a supposedly regular basis:

> *Ella and I draw from nature every Monday and Friday   On Friday I went over the creek, and she & I walked to Young's house (the one in which the McCalls used to live) we each took a view of it, Ella's was very well done—I expect Ella over today to draw M^r McCalls house on this side of the creek—* [s to h, 8 may 1825?]

Three years later the routine continued, but with less regularity:

Once a week, when the weather permits, Ella comes over to draw with me, as My Aunt hoped thus to give her some encourage-

ment. But I fear it does her very little good, as she never will draw at home, and once a week, even if she would come regularly,

is too little to improve much. . . . [S to Ev, 11 January 1828]

Eleu's talent for landscapes unquestionably surpassed that of the others in the sketching parties. Sophie experienced personal frustration with her own efforts but recognized her sister's superior ability to draw familiar structures and views in the neighborhood. Tat's sketchbooks have survived in part, and a few of Sophie's landscapes. It is curious to compare the two, especially on the rare occasions when they show the results of a single outing during which the girls sketched the same view. Invariably they emphasized different features of the sight before them, and invariably their perception of foliage, of lights and shadows, differed. But their application to the task was constant.

Although Sophie's real satisfaction came from her carics, and the landscapes were secondary, she enjoyed the camaraderie of the sketching parties. When Tom Smith came courting Tat in the summer of 1828, he happily joined them. Tom's presence, and the touch of romance, sparked renewed enthusiasm among the young women. One afternoon, at a favorite spot in a clearing, as Tom and Tat seated themselves to take a view of the factory, Sophie began a sketch of them from the vantage point of a rocky promontory. To her surprise and consternation, she discovered that Tom was taking a view of her—the only surviving sketch of the young caricaturist drawing from nature.

Regrettably, not all the sketches of Brandywine landscapes are signed or dated, and it is not always possible to identify the artist. Their value to Sophie, however, is made clear by her inscription in the one sketchbook that can be identified as her own, penciled years after the drawings were made:

Oh native vale! by all remembrances of childhood, by all joys of youth made dear—SMDP

Thomas Mackie Smith.
Drawing in the Clearing.
1828. Ink, 4 x 5⅛".